A WOMAN ᴊ

the transformative journey
from hurt to happiness

First published by O Books, 2008
O Books is an imprint of John Hunt Publishing
Ltd., The Bothy, Deershot Lodge, Park Lane,
Ropley, Hants, SO24 0BE, UK
office1@o-books.net
www.o-books.net

Distribution in:

UK and Europe
Orca Book Services
orders@orcabookservices.co.uk
Tel: 01202 665432 Fax: 01202 666219 Int. code
(44)

USA and Canada
NBN
custserv@nbnbooks.com
Tel: 1 800 462 6420 Fax: 1 800 338 4550

Australia and New Zealand
Brumby Books
sales@brumbybooks.com.au
Tel: 61 3 9761 5535 Fax: 61 3 9761 7095

Far East (offices in Singapore, Thailand, Hong
Kong, Taiwan)
Pansing Distribution Pte Ltd
kemal@pansing.com
Tel: 65 6319 9939 Fax: 65 6462 5761

South Africa
Alternative Books
altbook@peterhyde.co.za
Tel: 021 555 4027 Fax: 021 447 1430

Text copyright Dena Michelli 2008

Design: Stuart Davies

ISBN: 978 1 84694 087 3

A CIP catalogue record for this book is available
from the British Library.

Printed in the US by Maple Vail

O Books operates a distinctive and ethical publishing philosophy in
all areas of its business, from its global network of authors to
production and worldwide distribution.

No trees were cut down to print this particular book. The paper is
100% recycled, with 50% of that being post-consumer. It's processed
chlorine-free, and has no fibre from ancient or endangered forests.

This production method on this print run saved approximately
thirteen trees, 4,000 gallons of water, 600 pounds of solid waste,
990 pounds of greenhouse gases and 8 million BTU of energy. On its
publication a tree was planted in a new forest that O Books is
sponsoring at The Village www.thefourgates.com

A WOMAN'S WAY

the transformative journey
from hurt to happiness

By Dena Michelli

BOOKS

Winchester, UK
Washington, USA

Trust me; this book could save your life. I was hooked from the first line. Gentle, wise and compassionate, Dena takes you by the hand and takes you on a journey that will change you forever.

Erin Pizzey, international author, poet and playwright and founder of the refuges for women and children who have been subject to domestic violence

Dena shows remarkable humanity in her perception of a woman's dilemma and a remarkable ability to see the synchronicity which pulls a universal strategy out of each of their narratives. What I think is really enlightening about the book is the way she takes the individual circumstance – a silk thread if you like – and instead of simply setting it up as a separate case, she takes the individual strands and twists them into an elaborate, thick, silken chord so that each one contributes to the strength of the whole. She extracts from each individual case a strategy of wisdom.

Michael Glickman, architect and author

This book is both an emotional and intellectual inspiration to those who have experienced the pain of feeling unloved and abused. It provides a female perspective on what it feels like to have lived through such events and also on what it takes to overcome the past. The author uses her own experiences and that of her contributors sensitively to highlight the ups and downs of the journey towards healing while providing a range of stages required to overcome the legacy that such events leave. Academic rigour and compassion come together.

Gladeana McMahon, Fellow of the British Association for Counselling, Association for Coaching and Co-Director of the Centre for Stress Management

"A Woman's Way" is an experience, a friend, and an inspiration to guide women who desire to make positive changes in their lives. In fact all women can learn from it, even those who have not been touched by trauma but are simply experiencing change. Dena's writing is eloquent, personal and helps the reader understand emotional experiences and options for change. **Lynne van Brakel** is a facilitator of personal and professional development and a life coach

Dena offers the sincere reader an outstretched hand with which to journey; a journey from despair and confusion to understanding and the blossoming into the fullness of being. From the first chapter I could feel the invitation to go much deeper so I entered the book and experienced it fully. As I did so, it created all sorts of emotions in me. I really liked her writing style and even laughed out loud in places! There is an appealing 'dryness' to her humour which made me smile in spite of the challenging nature of some of the messages. It is a much needed guide, support and most of all, a gesture of loving understanding and encouragement. I would recommend it to all women who are making conscious steps from healing to wholeness. **Jay Keshava** is the co-founder of a holistic retreat centre in Glastonbury

CONTENTS

I dedicate this book to the twelve women who recounted their healing journeys and provided me with the data for my PhD research. I will always be inspired by their dignity and their generosity in helping to bring understanding forward.

I also dedicate this book to my grand-daughter, Zoë-Hope, an angel incarnate if ever there was one. By gaining greater understanding, I am hopeful that she will transcend the family pattern and live her life freely and fully.

PREFACE

I come from a family of wounded women. This wounding has been passed down the female line for at least five generations. And, from my growing perspective, as I advance through my own healing process, I realise that this wounding is likely to get worse unless something is done to stop it.

Trends seem to take on a life of their own when they are free from knowing eyes; and knowing eyes don't often penetrate the unexpected. So, in what appears to be a loving and successful family, wounding is not considered possible. Yet it is exactly this notion of 'impossibility' that gives rise to the private and secure conditions that are necessary for wounding to exist. And, in this fecund space, bounded by the unthinkable, the pattern of wounding can take on a life of its own and replicate itself like any other living, breathing organism. If, I argued to myself, this trend was to be arrested in my family; it must be exposed, explained and stopped. By pulling back the veil of ignorance and exposing the bones of innocent collusion, the inbred susceptibilities to wounding would be disabled. This done, the successive generations of women in my family would be free to live and love wholeheartedly. A heady motivation perhaps, but thus my journey began and, although there is no end to the journey of transformation and growth, I reached a stage where I felt suffi-ciently healed and motivated to research this process and share my findings. The research became the subject of my PhD. *A Woman's Way* is my sharing.

Sadly, childhood wounding is common. Studies on sexual abuse have shown that between one fifth and one third of women have experienced abuse as a child. This is considered to be a conservative figure as many do not discuss or share their experiences. Of course, men are not immune and their need to heal is every bit as great as women's. However, by all accounts, their number appears to be much smaller and, as only women volunteered for this study, I cannot really speak for men; although they may find real value in the findings. Nevertheless, as a result of the twelve women coming forward to share their healing journeys, this study has become one of the few that has been done by a woman, on women, for women. Most have been done by men, on men, for men. These male studies have long been considered to be the 'norm' so their findings are freely extrapolated to include women. When it is found that women don't conform to these all male models however, instead of being considered differently or uniquely gifted, women are considered to be deficient or abnormal!

On the matter of relevance to a wider audience, psychotherapists, John Firman and Ann Gila[1] in their book *The Primal Wound,* suggest that everyone suffers a primal wound, 'a violation by a significant other in which we are treated as objects, not as unique human beings'. This experience in the early years of childhood often results in a sense of anxiety or impending doom underlying everything we do or a sense of estrangement, falseness and lack of meaning. It can also result in fear of intimacy and an inability to form committed relationships. They emphasise their point by saying that the mixed and various cultures within which we live, which judge gender, colour and creed, create the conduits for this wounding. As do our early attachments to wounded carers who unwittingly pass their baggage down the line. '....and it cuts us off from the deeper roots of our existence.' It is to these 'deeper roots' that the transformative process described in this book encourages us to return.

In the last twenty or so years, child abuse has moved from being a taboo topic to being on the agenda of health authorities, social services and educational institutions and it is increasingly the subject of government attention and legislation. Media coverage includes high profile cases which draw much attention, both in the celebrity world and in society generally. As I write these words, news has just been released of the conviction of a man who took a six year old child from her bath, sexually abused her and left her naked in a back alley near her home. It always shocks me that these things are still happening to such young children. It is likely to take a long time before the repercussions of this act will be felt by her and it is likely too that it will take a great deal of courage and determination for her to overcome it. This is a cruel sentence to impose on one so young; a real unexploded bomb.

When the issue of sexual abuse was first voiced publicly, outrage followed the shocking revelations of its prevalence and many called for preventative and punitive action at the highest level. This did not fall on deaf ears and both crime and punishment became the focus of public interest. Action was seen to be taken in a number of widely broadcast cases and the public exercised its voice in exposing and condemning the perpetrators. Although some errors were made, at least decisive steps were being taken towards addressing this massively difficult and complex societal problem; one that was, and is, perceived very differently across the culturally diverse settings within which we now live.

Protection may have been won for some children as a result of the subject of abuse being raised and discussed openly and there may be hope for a large number of other children in the future. But sadly, not for all. There are still many who will encounter abuse as children and suffer its long term effects; and there are still those who carry the legacy of abuse. However, it seems that efforts to deny, excuse or tolerate the sexual victimisation of children have run out of steam. Breaking the taboo and making the 'un-discussable' discussable was the first step. Now we are fluent in the language of abuse, increasing numbers of people are choosing to take the healing journey in the hope that they can breathe new meaning into their lives and adult relationships.

My personal motivation to enter this territory is clear, but it is not only based on personal experience, it is also based on the belief that life is too short for any of us to be held to ransom for something 'bad' that happened to us as children. The world has much to offer and it is clear that we must dissolve the beliefs and behavioural patterns that prevent us from living our lives fully and joyously. The final impetus to my motivation, however, was provided by the arrival of my grand-daughter, Zoë-Hope, who came into this world with such a leonine roar of innocence and beauty that my interest in this issue was raised to missionary proportions.

I was also assisted in my mission by hearing the stories of a dozen courageous women who journeyed from a place of trauma to a place of hope and joy; from hurt to happiness. These women comprised the research pool that informed my doctoral research into transformative healing. In simple terms, it is the process of becoming fully expressed; a process of unfolding that leads to finding personal truth. Each woman gave her time freely and spoke openly and frankly about the ups and downs of her personal transformation. And, as a result of commitment to her health and her truth, each succeeded in transforming her pain into meaningful experience. This freed her from playing out her childhood patterns and enabled her to achieve success and hope for the future.

In each case, the women that contributed to this study had been physically, sexually and/or psychologically abused. In every case, this abuse had taken place in the family setting and very often this was in the home. Yet generally, in spite of the many dysfunctional, broken and single parent homes in existence today, the home represents security, stability and a safe harbour of love and support. We 'know' this to be the essence of family because our societal and cultural values tell us so; even if this view of the family sits at odds with what we experience. Being abused in the heart of the home; the place where you naturally expect to be safe, leads to confusion as we will see. This confusion binds love to abuse and creates a double helix of expectation and acceptance. You have to suffer for love.

I should perhaps stress that *A Woman's Way* is not about the twelve women who formed the backbone of this research. Instead, the thoughts and reflections that have been harvested from their experiences will be offered to the reader. In this way, those who have been wounded, as these women had, and who are seeking healing and happiness, as these women did, will be able to tap their wisdom and make use of some of their ideas.

Although many people may be interested in what happened to these women as children - perhaps so that they can identify with their experiences or be inspired by the magnitude of their transformative journeys - their stories will not be told in detail in these pages. I am not going to be revealing more than the merest essence of their information here. My reasons are as follows: Firstly, they wanted their anonymity preserved and, if I told their story in full, it would risk identification by those that knew them. Secondly, in each case, they preferred to transmute the drama of their pasts into something useful for others and this could not be done if they placed their feet back in their childhood shoes and relived their traumatic experiences in order to have them relayed here. Thirdly, because they had experienced transformative healing, there was no value in regurgitating old memories or engaging in further discussion about it. And fourthly, it was their intention that this book be forward looking and optimistic. If there was one message they hoped to disseminate through this work it was this; the future is of our making. If we step forward in self-belief we can create our own future and live our lives as we choose. Having said that, they do not take issue with the fact that this journey is a challenging one, and that there are almost as many steps backwards as there are steps forward. But the sum, as they so clearly demonstrate, ends with a powerfully positive integer.

By focusing on the journey that each woman took as she steadily stepped away from the aftermath of her childhood experiences, clarity about the stages of the transformative process emerged. And, when they saw the distillation of their experiences expressed as a route map, it was their wish that it should be published so that others, following the same path, might do so with more elegance and efficiency than they judged themselves to have done - and with less fear and uncertainty. It goes without saying that it is testimony to their efforts that the mysteries of this transformative process have been revealed and that this book has been written.

Sharon, one of the women volunteers who had been serially abused by her grandfather throughout her childhood years, said:

'If somebody had told me at the beginning of my journey that it didn't matter how long it took, and that it didn't matter what I did, but that I would get better, then that would have been great. That would have been enough. But if at the beginning, I'd been able to pick up the phone and speak to myself as I am now, then that would have been quite wonderful. I know you can't do that but that's what I would have liked.'

I hope that this book will have the same effect as being able to pick up the telephone at moments of challenge and speak to yourself at a time when you are feeling healed, happy and confident in your life. It is both a pro and a con that nothing stays still; the process of transformation is proof of this fact. It carries you from pain to pleasure and, if you trust it, it does so with the minimum of discomfort and the maximum of ease. This is not to diminish the journey, which will inevitably have its challenging moments, but these will pass and a brighter future will show itself on your horizon. This is, perhaps, the only thing you can be sure of.

Although this book is derived from the material presented and examined in an academic framework, the style and disciplines of academe have not been slavishly reproduced here. Reference to others' work has been included only when it adds something of value to the text. In addition, the complexities of the academic language have (hopefully) been dropped in the interests of a 'good read'.

Dena Michelli
April 2008
www.denamichelli.com

ACKNOWLEDGEMENTS

Firstly, I must acknowledge the twelve women who assisted me in this important project. You know who you are. I am truly indebted to you, as no doubt many others will be who follow in your inspiring footsteps.

I also owe a great deal of thanks to my husband, John Hobson. He demonstrated tireless belief in my research and writing as I swung from despondency to elation. At all times he was thoughtful, steady, supportive and gracious. And he built me a fabulous website!

My family were patient and supportive as I wrote, and wrote, and wrote. My mother came with me, bravely, as I recalled my childhood challenges. She also shared stories of her own troubled past and talked for the generations that preceded her from memories that came down the female line. My older sister, Pippin, pooled many of her own memories with mine and we walked a great deal of this path together. Over a period, we thought, talked and held each other a lot. My younger sister, Cherry, an epileptic writing about her experiences of this affliction, met me on mutual territory where we shared our writing frustrations and gave each other encouragement. She also provided sorely needed humour when things got a little intense. My daughter, Verity, my son, Benjamin and my father, were all loving holding forces even though they neither understood what I was doing nor why I was doing it. There were times when I was grateful for the distraction of grandmotherhood when Zoë-Hope and Michael came to stay. There's nothing like a nursery rhyme or a fairytale to get you back on track.

I have been fortunate in the people that have supported me as the book neared completion. Those who gave me valuable feedback included close from friends and virtual acquaintances who were introduced to me through my network. Erin Pizzey was so generous in her willingness to support this work. As a woman with extensive practical and political capability, she changed the face of the world for abused women. Gladeana

McMahon was rapid in her response to me and her support of the book. She was always professional, personal and generous. Thank you to Lynn Macwhinnie for putting her my way and to Hannah Greenwood, for putting Lynn my way. I am truly grateful for this connection. Lynne van Brackel, a dear colleague and friend took time to read the pages through intelligent appraising eyes and encouraged me to be more courageous in my disclosures to 'round out' the book. Jay Keshava, an inspiring entrepreneur and long-standing friend has created safe territory for those who are exploring their inner worlds, and she welcomed me into that space unconditionally for as long as I needed. She and I have ventured a great deal together and have seen our respective landscapes change so much compared to what we see today. Michael Glickman, architect, inventor, researcher, writer and friend. Steeped in the mysteries of the corn circle phenomenon, he raised his head and embraced my writing thoughtfully, providing a valuable perspective as a man and feedback that enriched the line of the book. And Carolyn from Kindred Spirit. The architecture of the book changed as a result of your incisive comments. Thank you so very much.

I must include grateful thanks to John Hunt, the man that sits at the centre of O-Books orchestrating this massive, complex and unrelenting publishing business. He offers hope and opportunity to many new authors and it is through his vision that expansive works are now more available to those who seek. His team, are fabulous too. Maria Watson; thanks for organising the Mind Body Spirit workshops. I know how trying these events can be to put in place.

Ed Org's artwork has enhanced this book immeasurably. I would like to acknowledge and celebrate his artistic talent, his willingness to be associated with this book and his patience in waiting for this project to come to fruition. If you love his work as much as I do, please visit his web-gallery at http://www.sirengallery.co.uk/

INTRODUCTION

The most frightening thing for many writers is a blank page or screen onto which her words are supposed to tumble. It is hard to know where to start. I guess the best thing is to invite you to join me for as long as it seems helpful and judge for yourself whether I can offer you anything of value or not.

If you have picked up this book, you may have been attracted to the implication that there is a dynamic force in women that offers something more than she is currently experiencing. You may have experienced abuse as a child or felt locked into patterns of behaviour that frustrate your happiness and thwart your sense of fulfilment. You may also have picked up this book because your work brings you into contact with those who are 'working on themselves'. Whatever your reason, I hope that you will find the time spent with me helpful and promising.

As a PhD graduate, I have been left with a considerable amount of academic baggage which I hope I have managed to relegate appropriately. I don't think this book will have lost anything by not following the traditions of academic writing and I don't think you will lose anything by not being privy to the ins and outs of the academic process. What I am attempting to do here is to explain a transformative process using the tools and fruits of the mind, whereas the seat of its success largely resides in the heart. However, not wanting to 'throw the baby out with the bathwater', so to speak, there is a great deal that the mind can offer this process in terms of building understanding and identifying the reasons behind certain patterns of behaviour. So, what I am hoping is that you will enter the text heart-first and *feel* the resonances before looking for the 'logic' that underpins and underscores your feelings. This will create a bridge between the head and the heart and will prevent you from getting stuck in the (albeit fascinating) intellectual intricacies and complexities which may only get in the way of what is going on for you and why.

For me, it was a long and difficult journey to move from reliance on my head to trusting my heart; from making sense of the world by *thinking* about it to making sense of the world by *feeling* it. Yet, it is the heart that holds the richest messages in matters of learning and transformation. Using cold, dark, shapes on a page to communicate these messages is a challenge and, at best, they can only be inadequate representations of the depth and wealth of the transformative journey. However, they may serve to point the way to self-discovery. They may also provide you with a language that will help you express and make sense of your own experiences. Let's hope so. So, again, let me encourage you to enter the book feeling first, mind second.

Although I have explained why I am not going to go into the women's stories in any great depth, I have not explained my own position on this level of intimate sharing and you may be wondering what happened to me to propel me into this work. You have read that abuse in my family was passed down the line like an heirloom but I have only hinted at the experiences I had as I took my place in the generational queue. Like the women in this study, I am not going to go into the details of my childhood past either nor am I going to risk the pull of the backward glance distracting you from the positive messages in this book, but perhaps I should say something to allay any speculation.

I choose to work with a community of people that had been sexually abused because I was working through the after-effects of a similar history myself. Aged five, I was abused by a regular visitor to our home. Although this person was known in the local community to be a danger to young girls, he was nonetheless welcomed under the guise of non-judgementalism and Christian generosity. Perhaps he was trusted too because it was inconceivable that such trust would not be honoured and rewarded. This is like giving an alcoholic access to the drinks cabinet and thinking that, because you have shown such generosity of spirit and trust in the goodness of their soul, they will meet your expectations and validate your faith. It is a dangerous game and one that is elaborately (yet unconsciously) set up to confirm your place on high moral ground. And, when they take the drink, you are affronted that they 'let you down', when perhaps it is the other way around.

However, while the visible impact this had on me was a long time coming, it became apparent in my adult relationships that I was unable to manage my boundaries and had few resources to make choices and assert myself. In dealing with this, I must say, that I have been blessed with a loving circle of friends and some excellent practitioners who helped me - and who are still helping me - work it all out. In addition to my boundaries being inappropriately invaded as a child, my mother, her mother and her mother's mother, all had 'stuff' like this to deal with. Sadly, my daughter too had her trials. Strong men with strong needs and a weak resolve. What a Molotov Cocktail! As a result of all this, we became strong women; survivors, but damaged.

So, this book is about a process of transformation and change that happens, in this instance, to be rooted in the history of abuse. On the basis that it can't get much worse than that (although this is not a challenge) if it is possible to find a fulfilled and joyous life from such a start, anyone can do it from anywhere, whatever their challenges have been. So whether you have stubbed your toe on a personal, professional, career or life issue, the possibilities of an alchemical transformation are bound to be wrapped up in your experience. And, with such a truth, you are bound to be able to find wholeness and happiness as you move forward.

Let me take you through the architecture of the book:

I have started by describing the experiences and thoughts I had when my grand-daughter was born. I was just 42, a significant age in cosmic terms! She became the impetus to stop the family pattern.

I go on to describe the way we make meaning. This is important because our meaning making activities create a psychological framework through which we see and make sense of the world. If this is incorrectly built at the outset of our lives, it can distort our ability to interpret what is going on around us. In the transformative process, it is this psychological framework, or part of it, that is dismantled, reworked and put back together again.

The ensuing chapters will introduce you to the different stages and features of the transformative process of healing. At the end of each chapter, some ideas for moving through the process will be included. Linda, one of the women who volunteered for the study, named them the 'saving graces'. The saving graces, therefore, are thoughts, suggestions or resources that may be useful to someone at a particular stage of the transformative process and, as the transformative process carries the expansive qualities of flowering, radiance and joy as symbolised by The Three Graces in Ancient Greek mythology, it seemed appropriate to adopt this term. Largely, the saving graces have been gleaned from the women who contributed to the research, but I have added some of my own for good measure. There are bound to be many more good ideas, tools and techniques that will provide you with the necessary equipment to move through the process efficiently so I suggest that you keep yourself open to other inputs in case they hold a key for you.

I have revealed a process that is depicted in two dimensions but please bear in mind that this is not the full story. Although the stages do generally proceed in the order given, they are not strictly linear, one following neatly from the other. In fact, it is common to bounce back and forth in a general forward direction; one step forward, two steps back, three steps forward. This is the nature of change. As you move through the process, your vantage point will change and the way you see your past and your future will change too. This may mean revisiting some of the stages that you feel as if you have already passed – but you will do so differently and with a different outcome. I will reiterate this dynamic later in the book.

If you would like to trace the transformative path with your finger as you reflect on each of the stages, please do so using model below as your guide. It will give you an overall picture from the outset. It may also give you a sense of where you are on the journey and where to dive into the text if you want to skip the detail behind one or two of the stages.

Continual process of healing – "I just get better and better."

Stage -1 Unawareness	Stage 0 Waking	Stage 1 Connecting	Stage 2 Disintegrating	Stage 3 Finding voice and Being heard	Stage 4 Meaning-making	Stage 5 Controlling	Stage 6 Integrating	Stage 7 Transcending
Denial	Physical illness	Recognising coping strategies such as:	Descent into chaos/the abyss	Seeking help	Making connections	Managing relationships	Sense of Self	Seeing things from a different perspective
Disassociation	Daughter at the same age that abuse was experienced by the mother	Denial	Falling into a black hole	Being 'witnessed'	Seeing the patterns and linkages	Controlling boundaries	Sense of completeness, wholeness, oneness	No longer identifying with the abused child
Compartment-alising	Death of a parent	Disassociation	Being fragmented	Being heard	Reading	Making decisions and choices	Feeling healthy	Focusing on the present and being optimistic about the future
Living on two levels	Re-abuse	Compartment-alising	Coping strategies not working	Being believed or validated	Training	Confronting abuser(s)	Feeling healed	Feeling elated
Displacement activities	Similar context	Living on two levels	Everything falling apart	Building a trusting relationship	Talking to others	Saying 'No'	Feeling powerful	Feeling joyous
Creating fantasies	Chance question or reflection	Displacement activities	Experiencing 'madness'	Being 'held' in the process	Finding different perspectives	Re-organising the home environment	'Inside' has joined the 'outside'	Feeling powerful
Suppressing memories	Body memories	Creating fantasies	Feeling depressed	Telling the 'story'	Re-sequencing the memories	Changing hair/image	Self-knowledge	Feeling in control
Intellectualising	Flashbacks	Suppressing memories	Overwhelming feelings of guilt, shame	Speaking out	Dropping into stillness	Venturing out	Purposeful	Optimism/ hope
Latent healing	?Stage of maturity	Intellectualising	Feeling anger	Finding voice	Silencing the mind	Taking chances	Increasing wisdom	Confidence
		'Ah ha' moments		Articulating the subjective and making it objective	Giving form and structure to past events	Being rash or reckless	Big picture understanding	
		Dread/fear					Embracing paradox and contradictions in terms	

Ongoing, iterative process between and within all categories

A Woman's Way – The seven stage transformative journey from hurt to happiness.

BIRTHING THE IDEA

This is how I remember the day that Zoë-Hope was born.

It was a sunny Sunday morning in August and Zoë-Hope had given her mother undisputed signs that she was ready to arrive. Dave, Zoë-Hope's soon-to-be father, was at work so Verity, who was vastly pregnant and somewhat overdue, called her brother Ben, who happened to be home from University and staying locally with an old school friend. Ben was, I think, somewhat alarmed. He knew that activity was required but he wasn't sure what form it should take. I think this fact amused Verity who always liked to get 'one over' her brother.

I was separated from all the activity by at least two hours by car but this is no time in the matter of a birth. Dave was happy to take his time returning home as he knew from past experience that babies don't often do things in a hurry. However I was concerned that Verity was alone so while I rearranged my day, I asked Ben to drive over and sit with her for a while. It wasn't long before he and his long time school friend arrived at her house. Both were a little gawkish and unsure of what they should do. Ben called me from Verity's side.

"OK, I'm here. What do I do?"

"Well that depends on how she is. What sort of state is she in?"

"Well she answered the door and seems quite normal at the moment. She's now sitting beside me watching me talking to you. 'Cheerful' might even be the word to describe her!" His voice became distant as he turned towards Verity in response to a groan. "Oh no. What is it? What's the matter?"

"What's going on?" I say desperately trying to envisage the scene.

"I don't know. It looks like she's having a contraction. Oh God. Does that mean the baby's coming?"

"Not necessarily. Tell her to breathe through the pain they way she was taught in her classes. Look; tell her I'm on my way. I'll jump in the car now. I can't bear being so far away while all this is happening."

To Verity: "Mum says breathe through the pain. She says she's going to come over."

There was a short silence. "It's gone now. The pain's gone for a bit. Tell Mum not to come yet. Dave will be here soon and we'll call her when we know what's happening. It could all stop for all I know!"

Ben began to relay Verity's message. "Verity says…"

"Yes, I heard but I'm going to come anyway. It sounds as if she is well on her way and I'd like to be there to support her. It'll take me a couple of hours so will you stay with her until Dave or I arrive?"

"All right, but I don't really know what to do."

"Make her a cup of tea and keep her nice and relaxed."

"Yes, but what if something *happens*?"

"Well, it is unlikely that much will happen other than the pains for a quite a while yet. I'll get in the car and start driving. I'll be on my mobile. Don't panic. Just be supportive and make her cups of tea. She might want a bath. You could run it for her."

"Hurry up won't you?"

"Don't worry. I'm sure Dave will be home soon. If the pains get to be very close together, call him and get him to hurry up. Otherwise, just be there for her and do what you can. I'm setting off now. You've got the number?"

"Yes. I have to say I'll be glad when one of you is here!" Then, fearing the worst, "Drive carefully, Mum, won't you?"

By the time I had arrived, things had hotted up quite a bit and Verity and Dave had left for the hospital. Ben had established himself back at Kevin's house; grateful not to have had to do anything other than make the statutory cups of tea. Naturally, he was both relieved and happy to see Dave come home and take over. Wanting to be helpful and mindful of my worry, Kevin had offered to drive both Ben and me to the hospital. When we arrived, we could see the expectant parents walking round the hospital grounds. Verity was, by this time, very uncomfortable, but walking was what had been prescribed for her so off she trundled, stopping every now and then to let the pain pass whilst Dave rubbed her back and spoke soothing words.

Ben, Kevin and I established a base camp under a tree and offered words of sympathy from time to time as the other two passed us in their orbit. The grounds were quite pleasant; not brightly flowered but away from the main hospital and quite tranquil. After quite a considerable time, the pains started getting worse and we all thought that it was time to go in and put Verity in the hands of a midwife. Dave invited me to go too so that he could leave from time to time to have a cigarette. It was on one of those occasions that I sat by Verity as she lay in the bath, breathing through the increasingly frequent bouts of pain. For most of us, childbirth is not easy and, as the pains became more and more extreme, Verity, all twenty years of her, started to get a bit frightened and upset. This broke my heart. However much I may have wished, I could do nothing to take the fear and pain away from her and I knew that things would get worse before they got better.

As the pains became deeper and more frequent, the midwife came in and suggested that we move through to the labour room. Dave joined us there, smoke on his breath. I remember Verity pushing him away with a sharp retort. I thought he must have felt bad at that point but he didn't react. His concerns extended to his impending family only. The labour proceeded from this point very rapidly. I offered to leave so that Dave and Verity could go through this experience together but they both said I could stay. I had mixed feelings about this. I so wanted to be there but I didn't want to be intrusive. This was such an intimate moment. I also didn't want to see my daughter in such pain so I vacillated a bit, saying that perhaps it was best if I waited with the boys. Dave pointed to a position beside the bed and gave me a clear instruction to put myself in it. He had that way about him: bossy but kind. There was no arguing. I aligned myself to the inevitability of the experience. Dave and I established ourselves on either side of the bed. We held Verity's hands and tried to do whatever would be most helpful. There actually wasn't much we could do but we tried anyway.

My focus was drawn towards the midwife.

"Come and have a look, Verity's Mum, you can see the top of its head."

Oh no, I thought, I can't possibly look 'down there', it is years since I had such intimate knowledge of my daughter's body. Surely she would prefer it if I stayed up at the top end.

"Come on 'Mum', or you'll miss it. Look at all that black hair."

The midwife's insistence worked. This was a now or never moment. I quickly checked with Verity and with her agreement, moved down the length of her long body. I was the first to see the baby's head. Dave checked my expression, smiled and went back to stroking Verity's hair.

"Oh my God, I saw its head. It has tons of black hair. Just like you did."

"Urghhhh."

I tried to swallow back the emotion at the thought of the impossibility of my own child giving birth to her own child. Her pain swelled in my throat and tears collected along the rims of my eyes. If only I could do this for her. I looked across to Dave who remained intently focused upon his wife. He too was blind with tears.

"I saw its head!" I said again, unbelievingly. The miracle so often spoken about suddenly acquired new proportions. Even though I had given birth myself twice, I had not felt this awe.

"Breathe in, blow out. In, blow out. In. Blow."

"Blow darling." In the absence of being able to do anything particularly useful, what more could a husband say?

"I am bloody blowing!" Then, in the general direction of the midwife. "Is it nearly finished?"

She replied reassuringly. "Not much longer now. You're doing really well. Now I want you to pant, don't push."

"Pant darling," Dave repeated.

"I can't pant, I'm pushing. I can't help it, I'm pushing."

The midwife spoke in a consistently calm voice. She must have done this many times. "Try not to push, keep panting, Verity. Keep panting. There's a good girl."

"I'm pushing. I can't help it. I'm pushing!"

"Pant darling. Listen to the midwife." Dave was by this time, completely off his natural turf. As a nuts and bolts engineer, all he could do was repeat the instructions.

"I am listening, for God's sake. I just can't stop pushing!" Verity wasn't impressed.

The midwife ignored the exchange between husband and wife. "OK, I want you to push now. Breathe in. Chin on your chest and... PUUUUSH. Well done. And again. PUUUUSH."

"Push darling!" said Dave.

By now my throat had closed and I was holding my breath. I was crying as silently as possible and trying to smile encouragingly. Why is it that when those you love are in pain, you try to reassure them with a smile?

"Once more Verity... PUUUUSH."

I look away from Verity's straining face in time to see Zoë-Hope's tightly shut eyes and crinkled features meeting the afternoon sun. She did not cry immediately. Tears wash down my face. I loved her instantly and completely. I loved Verity instantly and completely too but that was no protection. I was filled with despair and hope; sadness and joy. Zoë-Hope was so beautiful and yet I knew that she had moved into our lives, carrying again, the genetic tapestry with its characteristic pattern.

After the customary snipping, clipping and tagging, Zoë-Hope was put to the breast. We stared silently for what seemed like forever. Remembering that Ben and Kevin were still waiting outside, I thought I had better go and find them and let them know that the baby had arrived. Frankly, I needed the space. I'm not sure why, perhaps it was to release the tension and allow the tears to roll unchecked from my eyes.

Everything had focused on the moment of birth and I needed time to take stock, think for a bit and assimilate the happenings of the last few hours. I walked slowly and breathed deeply. As it happened, they were not far away; in fact they were still sitting in base camp drinking coke and eating crisps and chocolate. Apparently this was all that was on offer on a Sunday afternoon in Nuneaton.

"It's a girl." I announced, voice quavering and eyes over-bright.

They both stood to attention. Neither of them had the remotest experience of this kind of thing.

"Is everything OK?" asked Ben. Then seeing the evidence of my emotional outpouring, "Are you alright?"

"Sure. Do you want to come and see her?"

"Oh, I don't know. I mean, is it OK?" Ben's reticence was endearing but see-through clear.

"Well I don't think Vee would expect you to go home without seeing your niece. Come on. I'll take you.

You too, Kevin. You're practically family after all."

Ben and Kevin sloped along in my wake, silently harbouring worries about blood and gore.

"… I mean, are we allowed? So soon?" said Ben.

"It all seems quite relaxed and they don't seem to be very busy so don't worry."

"Oh, OK."

At the door of the labour room, the boys stood back, each inviting the other to enter first.

"Well come on one of you." The midwife was brisk but amused.

Ben took the lead eventually and approached the end of the bed whilst looking his sister firmly in the eye. "Are you OK?"

"I will be when I have had a cup of tea! She's over there."

Dave was sitting beside the bed with the new arrival. He was staring down at her as she lay along the length of his heavily tattooed forearm, her head cupped in his massive working hand. He looked as if he was making a series of silent promises to her. Ben looked across to the scene.

"Is that her? She's so small."

"She didn't bloody feel like it to me!" Verity said, never one for a display of emotion.

"Would you like to hold her?" This was an act of great generosity on the part of the new father.

"Oh no. I wouldn't want to hurt her. I'll just look."

"Come on Ben. Just make sure you support her head. Here, sit down and I'll give her to you."

Ben took his niece gingerly but quickly settled in to the experience.

"Hey Kevin, look at this." Ben said proudly.

"I am looking. Amaaaaazing!"

"OK everyone, you can come back later." The midwife was back in control.

We left the new family behind to get fully acquainted with each other. All of us were moved by the experience but uncertain where to put it. It had been such a special day and I was so grateful to have been part of it. Did I ever really thank Verity and Dave properly?

We departed, falling over ourselves and talking all at once. It didn't matter that no one was listening. Each of us had our own story to tell and all that was important was that we heard ourselves tell it.

Zoë-Hope's birth was a momentous time on my own healing journey and it dropped me into a powerful meaning making process that helped me see the world differently. The birth process is literally the process of becoming manifest as unique and potential-filled beings. I wondered what was in store for her and I wondered whether my store had been fully utilised. Had I done all that I could with my life and how could I best serve her. Acknowledging that there was more to do, Zoë-Hope awakened in me a purpose that has burned since and provided me with a life vocation. And, although I didn't realise it at the time, she mirrored the process that I was to explore for myself, and for others, in later years.

THE TRANSFORMATIVE PROCESS

If you are reading this, you will necessarily be a member of the human family! As a result of your humanity, you will be bound to a natural inner impulse to grow, develop and express yourself uniquely. You can't escape this tendency. You can deny it, resist it, devise all sorts of ways to ignore it or get around it, but you can't possibly suppress it. Not for long. It lies within you. Always. It may take a lifetime for you to access your fullness, it may take many, whatever, it has unstoppable momentum and it cannot rest. And, once you believe you have found your fullness, there is more to come! The joy of this is that it will take you on your own journey to full expression. The curse of it is that when the going gets tough, no one can do it for you; for yours is your journey and theirs is their journey – and that can be so hard. This process that is driven by our subtle and hidden drivers is the transformative process of 'becoming'.

The process of becoming is littered with challenges at the best of times, and we often encounter obstacles along the way that result in feelings of failure; of falling short of what we could have done or been. Yet the extent to which we have been impeded in our growth by our wounding only serves to highlight the challenges that are to be overcome by those of us seeking full expression. If these had not been put on our path, then the possibilities that we were born with would not have been thwarted or dimmed. Perhaps then our worlds would have received us, expanded before us and allowed us to release our full potential unabashed.

Being wounded is like trying to run free whilst being harnessed; if not impossible, a great deal of strength is needed to overcome the constraints of the harness. But it is possible to do and the prize is great. Try seeing yourself fully realised. What would you be doing? How would you feel? How would you look? Go on. Be audacious. There are no constraints in the mind!

In this book, I will go through the transformative process in detail using the women's accounts of their healing to identify and illustrate the different stages of the process. But perhaps I should point out that that each person travels their transformative path in their own way and there are subtleties and undercurrents in each person's journey that may differ from those that the women in this study have revealed. This is not to say that the stages on the journey are not common in most people's experience, it's just that the landscape at each stage may look a little different. Each person's approach to the challenges they face is unique, yet the nature of the challenges are likely to be the same.

It might be helpful to view the process as you would a route map complete with signposts, hazard warnings and a description of the terrain. The map helps make sense of the journey but it is not the journey; it is merely a guide to reduce the uncertainty and bewilderment that you may feel and to comfort you in your periodic yet inevitable feelings of isolation and loneliness. As you read, therefore, see if the stages speak to you and try to relate your own experiences to those of the women talking through this book. In this way companionship, comfort and colour will be added to your process and it will be made more understandable and meaningful.

More will be said of the transformative process later but above all, I would like to champion the natural wisdom of this process and urge you to trust it as it unfolds for you. In the end, all it requires is that you let go and let be. It's as simple as that. At the same time, there are complexities that it may be helpful for you to know about. Nonetheless, however you enter the process, whether you let go and surf the waves or whether you fall in an undignified heap on the floor, the rewards are many and they don't stop with the first iteration; the gifts continue for as long as you step along the path to realise and release your essential being.

HOW YOU MAKE MEANING

Many people believe that this is not your only life; that you have lived many times before and that each time you live, you build on your knowledge and wisdom through first hand experience. During these many past lives, you focus on one lesson or one task that represents the purpose of your particular incarnation. Thus you refine and build your essential Self; the only enduring aspect of you as you continually move between being a disincarnate and an incarnate being. This cycle continues until you return to the Source, or Spirit; the ultimate letting go.

As you can see, this is a deep, complex and contentious topic and one that many great thinkers have presented in esoteric literature over the millennia. If you wish to explore it, I suggest you go to the texts that focus on this subject specifically. They are rich and create a much broader perspective for your life but for reasons of brevity and clarity I am not going to explore the notion of eternal existence here, other than to say that it can bring understanding and context to a process that may otherwise be perplexing. If this is too much to swallow, perhaps this belief will stand; that you are here to learn and grow and to develop your personality in line with your truth to fulfil your potential.

For the sake of argument, therefore, I will suppose that you are at your most pure when you are born, save the genetic tendencies that you inherited from your family line. From the first moment of your life, you begin to interpret and act upon the world. At first you do this in a naïve way. You cry, you get fed. You don't cry, you don't get fed. Simple cause and effect relationships. But as you get older, you use increasingly sophisticated processes to make sense of your observations and experiences. You may test the people around you to discover where their boundaries lie; you may provoke reactions and experiment with physical matter to determine what the 'rules' are and you may copy the responses and reactions of significant others to inform your own behaviour. All this is done in the context of your given nature; your personality. And so it is that layer upon layer of learning and experience builds up to create the 'lens' through which you see and make sense of the world.

In learning circles, this lens is called the 'meaning perspective' and it is considered to be made from a combination of genetic inheritance, family background, societal and cultural values. This cocktail is laced by your observations, learning and experience. The meaning perspective, therefore, is a mix made up of thoughts that are continually reworked and updated by your experience of life, which in turn, modifies the way you see yourself and the way you act. However, the meaning perspective is not 'who you are'; it is the means by which you understand who you are in your current circumstances. If as a child, your experiences were damaging or destructive, the wiring in your meaning perspective will have become crossed and the way you project yourself will be 'distorted'. You could say that you have become the victim of your own meaning-making mechanism; you are caught up in your own wiring. In this way, your essential and eternal nature, or your true Self, can get overshadowed or even completely eclipsed by the personality; that bit of you that is responding and reacting to the things that are happening around you, now.

The society in which you live conveys messages about what is 'right' and what is 'wrong'. These form the backbone of you meaning perspective. During childhood, a structure of family values is added. If this sits in opposition to the values held at the societal level, they become family 'taboos' and are not discussed, justified or explained. Instead, they seed themselves as contradictions in your meaning perspective, which confuse and undermine you every time the contradiction comes to the surface. Further, the experiences you had as a child as you advanced through the natural developmental stages of your formative years, will have added more layers of complexity to your meaning perspective. If you were unfortunate enough to be caught up in a transgression of one of society's rules, the inconsistency between what happened inside your home and what happens outside the home will have caused you to create a kind of logic that links the two in the most credible way possible; credible to you as a child who does not have the 'full story'. However, this is a false logic that was invented to accommodate the contradictions and force them into some sort of explicable framework. Such distorted logic is inevitably negative and may include believes like "I am a bad person."

False logic is created through making assumptions, leaps in abstraction or fantasy. All these techniques deny the evidence before your eyes but they enable you to live relatively easily with the contradictions. However, somewhere inside, there is a growing tension between what you 'pretend' to be true and what you 'know' to be true and, although it becomes increasingly uncomfortable, you look for confirmation and validation from others. For this purpose, you instinctively seek out those who see the world as you do and who will play their part in confirming the truth of your fabrication. Either this or your explanations get more and more complex and convoluted and further away from reality.

You will probably sustain this strategy for as long as possible because you know, intuitively, that to challenge it literally means turning your world upside down. But it is inevitable that there will come a point when you just can't prevent the dramatic realisation that you have created an illusion of coherence; things are just not they way that you have been seeing them. In such a meaning perspective, because the abstractions and fantasies are not built on a solid foundation, the whole structure is in danger of becoming unstable and tumbling down.

I am reminded of a nursery rhyme that I used to sing in my childhood:

There was a crooked man and he walked a crooked mile.
He found a crooked sixpence upon a crooked stile.
He bought a crooked cat, which caught a crooked mouse.
And they all lived together in a little crooked house.

Although this nursery rhyme is rooted in English history and has nothing to do with meaning perspectives, it nevertheless evokes a feeling of the inevitable perpetuation of crookedness. Once it starts, it gets everywhere!

Meaning perspectives are unique to each of us and are populated by deeply held beliefs. They allow you to make meaning from your experiences and, the longer they are held, the more robust they become and the more difficult it is to change them. You often hear older people say that they are 'too old to change'. What they perhaps mean is that they have invested so much, and for so long, in their personal meaning perspective that it has become unthinkably hard for them to dismantle it and think about the world anew. In this way, peoples' ability to review and rework themselves can diminish or cease altogether as they age. Yet meaning perspectives are constructed by thought, there is nothing physical and immutable about them. They are illusory, and so, changeable. But this is too simplistic.

Meaning perspectives are not only built through logical (or illogical) deduction, they are also infused with archetypal expectations, associations, feelings and emotions. Your personality is projected through your meaning perspective and the world knows who you are as a result of it. Disentanglement from your old meaning perspective is extremely threatening. Because you are so tightly identified with it, to lose it is to lose yourself; your very sense of being. This is the illusion of this particular psychological structure. Meaning perspectives are *not* you, they merely inform your actions and others' experience *of* you – but they are responsible for creating the meaning and the context that you inhabit, know and understand well.

The true being that you are can be hidden or imprisoned by the values and beliefs you hold, especially in cases where these have been formed in dysfunctional settings and have become distorted in some way. I like to think of a meaning perspective as a knotted mesh of silken threads that have been woven into a complex pattern as unique as your fingerprint. They carry the impression of delicacy yet they are so strong that they can prevent your growth for decades – or a lifetime. For this reason, I prefer to use the term 'meaning mesh' rather than meaning perspective. To my mind, it conveys the notion of an enfolding, capturing or even imprisoning fabric that is wrapped around you like a cloak. Not only is it possible to conceive the ease with which it can be removed, but also the ease with which thoughts, ideas and beliefs, like briers, can get caught up in it.

During your formative years, your parents or carers taught you how to conduct yourself and what social and behavioural mores to follow. Slowly, and bit by bit, they helped you weave the meaning mesh that colours your perception of reality - until your credulity is stretched so far that it collapses. This collapse may be triggered by a shock or a contradiction in truth that is so severe, you can no longer pretend that it makes sense. For sure, you can pretend that an irreconcilable pair of realties hold true for so long but there comes a point when you can't kid yourself any longer; the dissonance is too great.

Before any collapse however, those in close and intimate proximity to you, and those who have a vested interest in the perpetuation of your cooperative behaviours, will work tirelessly to keep the structure sound. They will know how to do this because they will have helped you to create your meaning mesh in the first place. Indeed, they will have gently wrapped it around you, so tightly, that you see and define yourself according to their (convenient) reality. This may have been motivated lovingly; to serve your purposes, or malevolently; to serve theirs. If it is the latter, you are innocently set on a life path which attracts certain life experiences. Your behaviours are in line with a certain set of (distorted) beliefs so those who share those beliefs, notice you and do all they can to enter the well-rehearsed but dysfunction dance with you. You know your steps. They know theirs. It goes a bit like this: If you believe you are no good, you behave as if you are no good and you attract those people who will treat you as if you were no good. In short, you get what you think; you fulfil your own prophesy.

Reinforcing your own meaning mesh is not a solitary pursuit. It takes someone else to endorse your logic and to reward your behaviours. And you, in turn, will reward that person for influencing you by reflecting back their truth and confirming them in it. This person, or this group of people, may be extremely powerful and it will probably be difficult for you to find your own boundaries in the presence of them – because they 'know' you and they know how to press your buttons. What's more, your influencers need you to 'feed' them, so to speak; they *want* you to reflect back their values, beliefs and behaviours so that they also feel endorsed and rewarded. So, they create small mirrors of themselves to deepen their own reflection and in your innocence, you enter the collusion. However, if their meaning mesh was created in trauma and is dysfunctional, they merely pass on their own distorted views. So, your meaning mesh becomes an extension of theirs and you end up manifesting their attitudes and behaviours and meeting their demands. It is in this way that family patterns and susceptibilities are handed down from generation to generation, along with the genetic code.

As well as being bestowed with a set of prescribed reactions to situations and events, your behavioural momentum gathers over the years and eventually becomes the determinant of your experiences. In effect, your behaviours begin to orchestrate your life; emphasising and evoking experiences that confirm the 'correctness' of the meaning mesh – until the experiences can no longer be contained by it. If you take this study as a case in point, the childhood experiences of the women created a meaning mesh that included abuse as a way of expressing 'love'. Love being the espoused glue that holds a family together. This rendered the women victims; people who were submissive to those in authority or power positions. Not only did they become susceptible to externally imposed controls but they actually sought (unconsciously) controlling relationships in order to feel validated and loved. However, these controlling relationships merely reflected the experience they had had as children when control and love were two halves of the same coin; indivisible and inevitable.

Staying for a moment with this notion that you create your own reality, let's see how it might work. If you think of every thought as a waveform that emanates from your mind and gets bigger as it travels through space, you can perhaps imagine many waveforms travelling through space looking for similar waveforms to connect with. If this is the case, at some point, one of your wave forms will meet its natural counterpart amongst the collective waves of thought that emanate continuously from all thinkers. The resultant harmony either creates substance and form (in the material sense – a baby, for instance!) or a co-operative dynamic where both parties tacitly agree to act out a particular set of behaviours. However, if your thought form is based on a distorted premise, it only becomes enlivened when it meets with a compatibly distorted thought form. It is in this distorted environment that you feel recognised and validated and it is then that your new and exciting relationship re-enters the familiar world of dysfunction and possibly abuse. Of course, this merely serves to reinforce your meaning mesh because the experience is in accord with what you believe to be true. This is why you so often repeat your relating patterns and find that your adult relationships reflect those that you had in your childhood. As abused children, we unwittingly seek those that wish to wield power and control over us. This may be financially, physically, emotionally, psychologically or spiritually. It is manifest in many forms and it can be extremely subtle. The resultant effect is the same. We find ourselves in the submissive position again with little or no authority to determine our own destinies.

Once the patterns are revealed, many women are appalled to realise that they have 'married their abusers' and that the behaviour of their partner reflects those that they encountered in childhood. But the point that you create your own reality is a good one. Once the scales have fallen from your eyes, you can actively create situations that are harmonious for you and conducive for the full expression of your potential.

The tactics that lead to influence and control are not obvious. If they were, they wouldn't work, for who in their right mind would voluntarily chose a dysfunctional relationship and respond to the call of an abuser for a victim? In fact, the pull on dysfunctional patterns can be incredibly subtle and complex. You may choose a different physical type, someone from different social circumstances or someone from a different culture, but whatever you do to outwit yourself, unless it is done in full consciousness, you'll just end up repeating your patterns. How many second long term relationships do you know that have ended in exactly the same circumstances as the first, even though all the obvious signs were encouraging at the outset?

Your meaning mesh is intricate and complicated and its weave is an elaborate tapestry of conditions, contingencies, caveats, impulses and yearnings. The faces that you show to the world in each of your roles, as a professional, a parent, a lover or a friend, represent one aspect of the meaning mesh, which may be in a different state of repair to the rest. In this way, you can function perfectly effectively on one level, say as a professional, whilst living as a dysfunctional twosome with a lover or spouse on another – that is, until one of you changes.

The Persona and Shadow

These different aspects of the Self were named 'persona' by Jung. Persona stems from the Greek and refers to a mask; not merely a face mask but a composite image that is presented for a purpose. A 'mask' is usually reinforced by a set of behaviours that include language, tone of voice, gestures and demeanour. The accepted boundaries of the masks are determined and agreed by our culture, so people generally know when to adopt them and how to respond to them. It is an unwritten rule, for instance, that intimacies are not overtly explored in professional settings (although they are often explored covertly!) and that certain rules of etiquette are adopted in regal, hierarchical or political situations. We use 'masks' as signals of our intention. They enable events to run smoothly and get round the need to renegotiate the rules of engagement on each occasion. Sometimes we over-identify with our preferred mask and believe that it is a true representation of who we are. In this case, we would carry our mask into every situation, whether it is appropriate or not, and expect people to react to us according to the accepted rules. Think of those that believe they are superior and behave in a selfish and arrogant manner in all settings; those that fall prey to their own PR and think they are above exhibiting consideration for others; the adult acting out the 'spoilt child' and believing they should be given priority and privilege. These are examples of personae that have been over-adopted and over-emphasised.

The other side of the persona is what Jung called the 'shadow'. It is the reverse of the persona, the part of ourselves that we like to keep hidden. Often, the shadow is judged by us to be unacceptable and when we see it in others, we criticise and reject it. In fact, not only do we tend to reject the shadow behaviours, but we also tend to judge the entire person and reject them in totality. We do this because they are reflecting something that we find distasteful and have rejected in ourselves and we can't bear to see these shadow behaviours acted out elsewhere. However, just as when you direct light onto an obstacle it casts a shadow, so does the persona cast a shadow, it is inevitable. There is no being without the shadow side or there is no being at all.

The relationship between the persona and the shadow is an important one to explore and befriend as the shadow not only carries what you may perceive to be the unacceptable side of your nature, but also the strengths and resources that will enable you to act appropriately when your persona is threatened. In the case of the women in this study, their shadow side, often anger, had been repressed as children because it was not safe to challenge those who had power over them. Indeed, it may well have endangered them. However, this 'unacceptable' side of their natures remained hidden in their adult years and, even when it was necessary to protect themselves, they continued to identify with the victim. So, out of the shadow can come their strength. The shadow can hide a multitude of blessings.

I don't want to dwell excessively on the psychological aspects of this process but it is useful to have some grasp of the subject so that a proper understanding may be gained from the research and its findings. It is, after all, the different masks that we wear that give people an experience of the person we project and it is the masks that determine their relationship with us. Each mask has been invented as a result of a belief we hold so it follows that an examination of our masks can lead to an understanding of the Self, and it is this deepening self-understanding that enables transformative healing to take place.

Making changes

The process of changing a meaning mesh can be a long one. Although there may be 'road to Damascus' flashes of enlightenment on the way, these merely facilitate another step towards the ultimate accumulation of steps and their eventual transformation into a larger, more integrated meaning mesh. There is much unravelling to do in the transformative process and it is rare for it to happen instantaneously. A small step at a time seems to be the order of the day, so celebrate each new realisation and change in behaviour. You'll probably fall back from time to time, but at least you'll be aware of this and your resolve to do differently next time will be hardened.

In the following chapters, I will explore in depth each of the stages of change and transformation and draw from some of the interviews to illustrate them. The stages may speak very personally to you and trigger some reactions that get you thinking more deeply about your own situation. If you feel vulnerable or uncertain about looking behind your own veil, it may be a good idea to ensure you have someone to turn to for support or somewhere where you can offload your perceptions and insights. A good friend or counsellor and a diary or journal are good ways of capturing your fleeting thoughts and making them manageable.

I have used pictures to portray what I believe to be the essence of each of the stages. Those of you who are more visual may find them helpful. Your intuitive response is likely to be the most meaningful. When I first saw them, I responded to them immediately. Their magical, elfin-like quality spoke to me of delicacy and possibility, reflecting the many fine-threaded manifestations of the meaning mesh. Both clear and complex, the drawings seemed to align themselves to the different stages quite naturally. I have also found some verse and a few sayings that complement and enhance their messages. I hope.

Here are some brief descriptions of each stage in the transformative healing process which were identified through the women's testimonies. It may help to orientate you towards the dynamics of the process.

Stage -1 (Unawareness)

'Minus one' doesn't mean that you're not doing anything, but that what you are doing is habitual; you are not conscious of it. You are using old coping strategies to help you move through your life and make sense of your thoughts, actions and feelings.

Stage 0 (Waking up)

This is the point at which you are made aware of your behavioural patterns through a trigger. It is as if you are suddenly put into a position where you experience your strategies failing, perhaps through an incident or accident. This stage is often experienced as 'the wake-up call'.

Stage 1 (Connecting)

During this stage of the process, you are able to look back and identify your patterns in a more or less objective way. It is as if the scales have fallen from your eyes and you see yourself in a new light – not always a flattering one! To continue with your habitual responses now is a deliberate act of collusion and you cannot avoid taking responsibility for it. This stage is often called the 'ah ha' moment.

Stage 2 (Disintegrating)

Feelings of confusion and chaos are common to all models of transformation. They happen as you let go of your 'old' style of behaving. Transformation requires you to 'let go of the old' in order to 'give birth to the new'. It is a death and a rebirth; a process which may bring a sense of loss. This sense of loss is caused by you letting go of your former identity (perhaps a fantasy) before you have found a new expression which is more authentic. You draw upon the qualities of courage and resilience at this stage of the transformative process as you may find yourself floundering around as you try to make sense of what is happening to you.

Stage 3 (Finding your voice, being heard and validated)

When you enter the disintegrative stage, you often find the need to be seen, heard and validated. Being received in confusion, and sometimes in despair, is essential if you are to proceed. At this stage, you may find that you need to speak out your thoughts so that you know what they really are. A listening and non-judgemental ear is important at this point.

Stage 4 (Meaning-making)

Here, the limitations and inadequacies of your former worldview are recognised, deconstructed and reconstructed. You may find it hard to let go of old paradigms and accept that there are different ways of seeing or thinking about things. Your past influences and long held values and beliefs are often hidden from your conscious mind and can remain unquestioned for much of your adulthood. Meaning-making comes from thoughtful processing; from 'trying out new ideas for size' and arriving at new conclusions. You often need to retreat from your familiar world at this stage so that you can look at things from a different or new perspective without all the old triggers calling you back into your former responses.

Stage 5 (Controlling)

It is during the controlling phase that you are able to make active choices and stop giving your power over to another person. You may begin to define your boundaries more clearly or you may make completely new ones.

Sometimes, people seek those with whom they have had unsatisfactory relationships and confront issues that were avoided in the past. This enables them to clear the air, put things to rest and find closure. Some people set new rules and conduct their relationships on a different basis whilst others make changes in their living or working arrangements. Whatever or whoever you have been controlled by in the past, you are now more able to control your environment and your relationships.

Stage 6 (Integrating)

The integrating stage is when you weave new thoughts, ideas and behaviours into your worldview. By taking a fresh perspective on life you are effectively expanding your mind and adding to your behavioural toolkit. The integrating stage allows for the possibility that two conflicting ideas can co-exist. There is no more 'right' and 'wrong', 'black' or 'white', but a broader and more inclusive understanding of complexity and ambiguity.

Stage 7 (Transcending)

Finally you 'let go' of your old ways and experience a feeling of both separation and wholeness. You are separate from the pull of the past *and* you have fully integrated it into all that you are. Your focus of attention is now firmly in the present. So, you move from identifying with 'what was' to identifying with 'what is'. Sometimes this stage is accompanied by a physical sensation of movement. Whether this happens or not, you are likely to have feelings of optimism and joy when you have let go of the restrictive beliefs and practices that you used to hold so firmly.

Each person travels the transformative path in their own way and they will encounter challenges that are peculiar to their own process. However, whatever the precise nature of the stages, the fact of them is true for everyone. On the journey of transformation and change, the general geography is shared by everyone but the geographical features may look a little different to each one of us.

STAGE -1 – UNAWARENESS

And moving thro' a mirror clear
That hangs before her all the year,
Shadows of the world appear.
There she sees the highway near
Winding down to Camelot:
There the river eddy whirls,
And there the surly village-churls,
And the red cloaks of market girls,
Pass onward from Shalott.

The Lady of Shalott, Ed Org   **Alfred, Lord Tennyson – 1809-1892**

I chose this image because the Lady of Shalott is not allowed to look out of her window directly onto Camelot without befalling the curse that has been laid upon her. Just as abused children are not allowed to question their abuse or see it in a light other than the one given to them by their abuser, the Lady of Shallot is contained within four walls where her perceptions are merely reflections of reality. Her experience of all that happens beyond the room she inhabits comes from the forms and shadows that pass across her mirror. In the case of the abused child, her experience of what happens beyond the room is an illusion, fashioned especially for her by her abuser; her mirror on the world. This image conveyed to me the notion of existing out of consciousnesses in a world of supposition and illusion, yet protected, in one sense.

Coping strategies are formed when a recurring situation becomes too threatening or dangerous for us to use our 'fight' or 'flight' instincts. If you take flight, you're vulnerable and unable to survive and if you fight, you are bound to lose and evoke more trouble. Generally, it is the imbalance of power that steals the fight or flight options from you so, in order to survive, you have to find an alternative strategy, perhaps 'freeze'. Freezing demands that you stay put, so in your immobility, you develop a set of behaviours that ensure your survival on the physical, emotional, psychological or spiritual dimension – or all of them.

If a child is subject to unpredictable outbursts of violence or abuse, she might develop submissive or pleasing behaviours that minimise the effects of her maltreatment. She may also find ways of explaining or legitimising her perpetrator's behaviour that make her believe that she is 'a bad girl', an 'unlovable person' or even an 'unworthy human being' undeserved of love or life. Sadly, these tactics create psychological structures and behaviours that endure even when the necessity for them disappears; they become 'hardwired' or frozen into the psyche of the abused child and distort the way she sees and experiences the world. For observers in later life, these behaviours reveal the meaning mesh that she holds to be true; one that has become distorted by repeatedly poor experiences and one that creates and perpetuates the world as she knew it.

From an early age, Heather had been persistently sexually abused by her father and his close circle of friends. In order to survive, she learned to give her power away and, as a result, her adult relationships were coloured by men taking control. When she married, she chose a man who was emotionally abusive and restricted her access to money. Her husband also made a strong connection with her father who sanctioned and reinforced the domineering and diminishing approach he had to his wife. In order to distract herself from the severity of her situation, she began to clean the house obsessively and engage in other compulsive behaviours which became evident to her children. At first, Heather couldn't see the way her husband used her emotional and financial dependency on him to control her but as her children grew, they began to ask her what she was doing and why she was doing it. Even though they were young, they were perplexed by her compulsions because they could see that her behaviours didn't accord with those of their friends' mothers. When these questions came 'out of the mouths of (her) babes', Heather was forced to think about things in a way she hadn't done before and she realised that she had to do something about her situation.

Although, as a mother of small children, Heather wasn't in a position to make any immediate changes, she slowly managed to change her self-belief and gain more confidence. She did this by taking small steps in her professional sphere where it was safe to do so and where there was an escape route into familiar territory if she needed one. To begin with, and only occasionally at first, she started going out with her colleagues and, although she felt it was a relatively small thing, she found that she was making a much more powerful statement than she had at first thought. It was not just taking control from her husband that was so powerful but also holding her own in a widening social circle. By getting out of the house and putting herself in different situations, Heather began to trust herself more and those who were not family members. After a while, and knowing something of her restrictions, her colleagues encouraged her to spread her wings more by going to college to get a qualification. This was another form of liberation for Heather because once she returned to education, she realised that she could cope with the academic material; a notion she hadn't entertained before. Bit by bit, and over time, Heather began to take more decisions and continue to build her self-confidence. Although it was not always easy and unforeseen challenges sometimes got in her way, she was beginning to see herself differently and the perceptions that had kept her as a victim were slowly being eroded and changed.

When Heather was talking about this stage of her process, she recognised that her children had reached sufficient maturity to observe her coping mechanisms objectively. At the point they questioned her, they had seen enough outside the home to know that others didn't act in the way their mother did. So, we have several people on the development path interacting; Heather, with her old coping mechanisms and her children who learned to be more objective as they grew in maturity and autonomy. But it was not only the children that observed her behaviours; her colleagues also had something to say on her obsessive drives. Yet in spite of the fact that they were so noticeable to her close circle, Heather was unable to see them for herself until she received innocent and objective feedback from her children; the two people that mattered most to her in her life and probably, the only two people for whom she was prepared to change.

We create coping strategies to help us through particularly traumatic situations. In most circumstances, we dispense of them as soon as they are no longer required but if the trauma is sustained over a period of time, we embed these strategies in our behaviours and use them to help us deal with the world. What we are doing, subconsciously, is protecting the child in us that was threatened in the past and, even though our childhood threat has disappeared, we automatically resort to these behaviours as if it still existed. This creates a longstanding legacy that defines the challenge for healing and for reaching a healthy place of awareness and choice.

Coping strategies then, are the artefacts of our earlier experience and they inform the way we protect and defend ourselves. However, they become so engrained in us that we forget to question their long term usefulness and we faithfully carry them into our adult years where we live them out, even in the absence of threat. We do this because the messages that we were given in childhood had such a profound impact on us that they became drummed into our minds and into our behaviours. And, these messages were usually delivered in highly charged emotional environments that carried the threat of withdrawal of love, abandonment, violence, humiliation or shame. So, ignorant of their long-term impact, we continue to draw upon our coping strategies even though they have no obvious purpose; we don't stop fighting even though the battle has ended. We can perhaps define a coping strategy as a diversionary tactic or as a means of protection that deflects attention away from painful areas. Coping strategies substitute a threatening or painful situation with one that is acceptable or benign. If this diversionary tactic fails, the full extent of what is being avoided will be revealed and chaos will break out. On some level, we know that our coping strategies are protecting us form 'a fall' so we contrive not to visit a painful experience from the past because we don't want to be faced with dealing with it in the present. In fact, we often go into denial and avoid using our recall mechanisms at all. It is amazing that we can choose not to remember something and, over the years, we probably have got pretty skilled at not remembering what's painful. Or we use elaborations of the truth to make what was painful acceptable.

Heather talked about how, as a child, she spent hours and hours working people out and speculating on what was happening around her. When she found an explanation, she was content and able to find her place in the story. Then, when something happened that didn't fit her story, she'd go back to the beginning again and create another thread that would add to the plot. Each time she worked out a new thread, she was OK and, complex though it became, she found a way to live with her situation. This cycle repeated itself many times. When her story was blown away, she did not feel OK and she'd have to weave another explanation or create another elaboration so that she felt OK again. Looking back, Heather realised that she had done this all her life. If she was able to intellectualise what was going on, if she was able to create a theory from her observations, she could distance herself from the situation and see it as an interesting case study that belonged to someone else. But by living in her head, Heather was not accessing her intuition or using her instincts to inform her of what was going on. In this way, she missed the signals from her children and failed to see that she was not connected to them or the situation they were in.

I wonder if the natural dynamic of people growing together in a household necessarily brings the process of transformation into relief. Everyone is moving along their path and their perspectives are necessarily changing as a result of this. Perhaps it is only a matter of time before one person's new perspective leads them to question another's. In fact, it probably doesn't matter whether it is a family, a school or a community, the dynamic created by people living in close proximity is bound to bring challenge and change. If this is the case, nothing can remain the same or, if it does, it is only as a result of denial and collusion from all sides – not an uncommon situation in families where adopting 'the family code' is the only way of being and belonging.

As we move into adulthood and put ourselves out into the world, we take our old coping strategies with us thinking that they will serve us in the same way that they have always done. However, because we had to create them in the first place, and because we have held them for so long, we have deadened our ability to read situations and to respond to them in the moment. We are always rehearsing the likely outcome and responding to it as if it were fact. So, we experience life through a distorted lens and we superimpose more distortion as we observe and react to life from the perspective of our old coping strategies. What we are effectively doing is building life experience on the rocky foundations of our childhood meaning mesh, so we have to go there to check out its state of repair and replace some of the building blocks if necessary. Once we are on an even keel, we can start our journey in earnest.

Throughout the research, there was a sense that the process had a natural order and rhythm to it. The women's experiences and their comments suggest that everything happened as it should have. That there was wisdom in the way it unfolded for them. This may have been the nature of the process or it may have been the way that they interpreted the nature of the process. However, whether it is the process's wisdom or your own that guides you, you can be sure that the stages are metered out only when you can cope with them.

The Three Graces, Raphael circa 1503-1504

The Three Graces may also be known to you as 'The Charities'. They are usually considered to be the daughters of Zeus and the sea nymph Eurynome (or Oceanid) and are a trio of Goddesses that represent the qualities that are conveyed by their names. Aglaia (considered to be the youngest and most beautiful) – personifies the qualities of beauty, splendour and radiance; Euphrosyne personifies the qualities of joy or mirth, and Thalia, whose name means to flower or bloom, personifies the qualities of rejoicing and good cheer. The three graces were often found in the company of Aphrodite, the goddess of love, and they sang and danced to the music of Apollo on Mount Olympus. It was believed that they endowed artists and poets with the ability to create beautiful works of art. I am using the symbolism of The Three Graces to encourage women to flower into their radiance and joy.

Saving graces: Unawareness

Just as these coping strategies are unconscious at this stage of the process, so are the saving graces. In a sense, you are in a blissful (?!) state of ignorance during this period of the transformative process because you are not aware of the dysfunctional patterns that govern your life or, if you are, at some level you calculate that living with them is preferable to facing and changing them. Sometimes, as we reflect back on this period, we remember friends, family or foes making challenging comments about our behaviours that caused us to be indignant and shun their feedback. We may recall ourselves saying something like: "Why is it that everyone keeps telling me I'm angry!" or "What is it about me that makes people feel that they can tell me how to live my life!" For me, the retort that defined my 'unconscious' years was: "why do people keep accusing me of not believing in myself!" To be fair, this period of 'Unawareness' only reveals its truth with hindsight so don't judge yourself harshly or expect too much of yourself; just allow your awareness to emerge gently and notice the patterns without beating yourself up.

Intolerance of the length of time that you spent in your unconscious coping state generally emerges after the trigger has been experienced and brought you into awareness. Many people play the 'if only…' game. 'If only I had recognised these patterns when I was younger, then I wouldn't have wasted so much time in my dysfunction… in my relationship… in my job!' However, it is important to remember that you are where you are supposed to be and doing what you are supposed to be doing – and this was as true then as it is now. Although it may seem like a waste of youth and experience to you, the time you reside in unawareness is developmental; it lays down the foundation of your transformation. This is not wasted time, it is time spent in building up patterns that later become recognisable and actionable and it is time spent building strength in order to do this. I don't think there are many people who don't need a challenging history to provide the impetus for change. It is only by keeping on doing what we have always done and by keeping on experiencing the negative effects of our actions or reactions that we eventually wake up to ourselves and our lessons.

Once Heather returned to education, and realised that she could cope with the academic material and meet others on an intellectual basis, she began to take more decisions and build her self-confidence. Heather gives a good example of how her awareness was raised during a social work course that she attended. Until that point, she was unaware that she was avoiding looking at things. This raising of awareness acted as one of the triggers to her process of transformation and gives a good example of how some of these stages can go hand in hand.

'The theory that we were covering on the course suddenly started to trigger all this stuff that I'd always known, but had always felt that it was in the past and it was 'done and dusted' and that was OK. But I didn't know what was wrong with me. I just knew that I had reached the point where everyday going into college was a struggle; going into placement was a struggle. I was tired; I thought I was ill, it felt like I was ill. You know, all sorts of things seemed to be falling apart like I couldn't hold it together anymore and I still couldn't identify what was wrong and I wondered if... because I would listen to the theory slots and think, I know it, you know? I know this, this is not news to me... and being aware that it disturbed me and I was unsettled but not thinking it was having any effect.'

If you are reading this book and thinking that none of this applies to you, it may be worth putting it down for a while. Perhaps this isn't your time. However, it may also be worth looking back on your life and identifying the recurring themes that you have experienced. What are the familiar downhearted feelings that you encounter time and again, what is their nature, and in what contexts do they strike you most often? For some people, recognition of the need to travel the path of transformation dawns as another relationship crumbles, another job is lost or another financial disaster occurs. You may hear yourself say: "Why do I always go for men who drink too much?" "Why do I always end up being used?" "Why do I never have enough money?" or perhaps "Do I have 'mug' written in large letters across my forehead!"

You may be a rare and blessed person that manages to avoid such things, but most of us get those sinking feelings when we feel ourselves falling into a situation that we have experienced before. For me, it was bullying bosses. I suddenly realised that I was being bullied repeatedly by those in power over me. Of course, I would protest loudly to whoever would listen but I always seemed to end up with a boss who felt he could bully me. My indignant feelings gathered momentum until finally, my back gave way and I ended up in hospital with major surgery pending. It was then, as I lay helpless, that I looked back and asked myself what it was that had 'broken my back'. It was interesting that I reamined confined to my hospital bed until I had made a commitment to explore and reveal the dynamics that had put me there.

If you are having difficulty identifying your life patterns, ask someone who knows you well and who has observed you in most situations. Receiving this feedback may be challenging but remember it is a gift. It will help you on your way to taking greater control and living out your potential.

Awareness

There are three saving graces that will get you through the entire process of transformation. The first is 'awareness'; often referred to as mindfulness by Buddhists. Once you are aware, or mindful, you will be able to scrutinise your thoughts, habits and actions and put them into your meaning mesh where they may be judged as fit or unfit for your purposes. Awareness may be applied to every aspect of your life from the way you breathe to the way you live out your life purpose. Bringing awareness to your thoughts and experiences becomes a discipline that will keep you vigilant and enable you to make the necessary adjustments to keep you in control of your life and well served by it.

There are three books that helped me with the notion of awareness:

The Power of Now: A Guide to Spiritual Enlightenment by Eckhart Tolle

Mindfulness: Choice and Control in Everyday Life by Ellen Langer

and *Be Free Where you Are* by Thich Nhat Hanh

Intention

The second saving grace is 'intention'. It is in the light of your intention that your most appropriate and helpful decisions can be made. By following your intention, every decision you make or action you take will be aligned with what you wish to achieve. It literally enables you to manifest the future you desire or to create your own reality. If you think of someone who has no clear intention, they tend to dissipate their energy on lots of projects that go nowhere. They may also invest in relationships that don't serve them, or worse, relationships that put them on a destructive path. By bringing *awareness* to your *intention*, you can clarify the way forward and make the choices that will reward you in both the short and the long term.

You can use visualisation techniques to make your intentions clear and to bring them to life. Have a look at *Visualisation* by Shakti Giwain.

Attention

The third saving grace is 'attention'. By bringing attention to and placing your focus upon your intention, you are able to provide the energy and momentum to ensure success. This is the discipline that you bring to your manifestation projects. It reminds you where you are going, why you are going there and calls for the appropriate amount of energy to be directed to the best and most efficient effect. If your attention wanders and you are undisciplined in your approach, your energy will be spent in irrelevant areas and will become depleted, leaving little to manifest your intention.

Regardless of the trajectory of your life, it may be worth spending some time thinking about what you want to achieve. Try to identify the things that are important to you and set some goals around achieving them. The clearer the goal, the more likely it is that you will reach it. Common wisdom suggests that your goal's boundaries should be clearly defined and that you should be able to tell when you have reached it. Also, by putting a timescale on the achievement of your goals, you will be able to plan your way and take the decisions that need to be taken at the right moments. If you read between the lines of the women's testimonies, you will notice that their driving principle was always to achieve a state of health, happiness and freedom.

Perhaps Deepak Chopra's *Seven Laws of Spiritual Success* will help you place your attention where it is needed.

Be audacious! Set challenging goals for yourself. If you surround them with limitations, ask yourself why you don't deserve the full extent of your dreams!

STAGE 0 - WAKING UP

For most people, presence is experienced either never at all or only accidentally and briefly on rare occasions without being recognised for what it is. Most humans alternate not between consciousness and unconsciousness but between different levels of unconsciousness.

Valkyrie, Ed Org   **Eckhart Tolle**

In Norse legend the Valkyries decided which deceased warriors had fought the bravest battle and then they escorted them to Valhalla where they would side with Odin to fight the final (end of the world) battle. This particular Valkyrie seems to be holding her breath in expectation of her work. Her eyes are shut, she may be rallying her internal resources, but she appears to have the qualities of dignity and courage; both helpful once the battle cry has been sounded – or the trigger experienced.

Waking up is when we open our eyes to what is happening in our lives. We see the reality of our world in Technicolor and it is not always the fantasy that we had ourselves believe! Very often, our waking is triggered by an event. Broadly, these include the natural movement from one growth stage to the next (adolescent to adult or adult to mid-life for instance) and those times when, out of the blue, life kicks us in the teeth.

Many people believe that although these events are both shocking and challenging, they also bring an opportunity to learn and grow. Life's crises have a habit of doing that. They present situations that don't fit into our meaning mesh and we have no immediate resources to make sense of them. The death of a loved one. An accident or illness. The birth of a child. Redundancy. A broken heart. All these things can be powerful triggers for reappraising things, conjuring up new perspectives and learning a new set of responses. So, perhaps we can say that a crisis is also an opportunity for growth; a trigger that propels us into a transformative process. I must stress here that I am not saying an essential ingredient of growth is pain, rather that with pain, comes the opportunity for growth. Of course, we are free to resist the opportunity given to us and no doubt you have seen examples of those who resist growth and live in pain as a consequence, as we too may have done in the past. However, the women in this book, along with countless others, have embraced their opportunities for growth and have sought to shed light on the deeper truths that their crises revealed.

Although the term 'crisis' is brutal sounding, we are blessed in so far as we can neither anticipate nor imagine what a crisis will look or feel like or when it will occur. If we could, we might step through life gingerly and fearfully, pulling back from every experience in case it was the one that would hurt and challenge us to change. Most of the women looked back on their transformative process with objectivity; like viewing it from a distant hill and looking down upon it with clarity and perspective. When interviewing them, it was as if they could access their memories but there was no emotional attachment to them; almost as if they belonged to someone else and they were just looking after them for a while. This is a phenomenon that will be discussed in the final stage of the process; the stage I have named 'transcending'.

Triggers are often experienced by women when their children reach the same age or stage as they were when they first encountered abuse or a life-denying crisis. This natural dynamic puts the transformative process on the radar screen to be dealt with or denied. But denial is not really an option now. When we feel fear for someone we love, we can't avoid the issue any longer. It is then that our willingness to take up arms reaches a crescendo and we go where we have been fearful of going in the past. There are many tales of mothers who have suddenly found enormous strength, physically as well as emotionally, when their children were threatened. They overcame their fears and phobias for the sake of their children and they endured hardships that most people would shy away from. Indeed, they very often sacrificed the expression of who they were in order to provide for their children.

The women I talked to often revealed that they had decided to enter the transformative process on behalf of their children. Perhaps this wasn't explicit at the time, but looking back, they realised this was why they did it. Perhaps they reasoned that they were not important enough to rid themselves of emotional baggage. Perhaps they felt that they had no right to be happy. Perhaps, they didn't think they had the strength or energy to enter the process for their own benefit. Whatever their reasoning, when they perceived that their offspring were susceptible to the same experiences that they had had, they garnered their courage and began their journeys. For me, I was very clear that if I did this, if I really started to go inward, I would, in some way, be able to prevent trauma from being passed down the line, generation to generation. If I could be healthy and wise myself, I could guide my daughter through this challenging terrain and give her the capability and confidence to deal with challenges when they arose – and she, in turn, would be able to protect her daughter. The daughters who triggered this response in their mothers were probably not under threat in reality. This wasn't really about them; it was about them inadvertently waking up their mothers by re-presenting one of the defining features of their abuse.

During the conversations with the women, the importance of hearing themselves speak out about their process became clear. Very often valuable connections were made and insights were gained through looking back and reflecting on their experiences. In a way, the conversations themselves were a sense-making activity that brought clarity and purpose to their journeys. This is just another sign that the process doesn't end. There is always another light to shine on what has happened and another layer to plumb.

Claire had been physically abused by a family member who was in a caring role. This contradiction followed her into her adult life and, unbeknown, she sought caring yet controlling relationships that disempowered her and 'kept her in her place'. When she married, she found someone who mirrored her childhood experiences and in the same way that her survival had been traded with abuse and control as a child; her husband also traded her survival with abuse and control. Claire didn't question this in her early marriage because her husband's behaviour merely reinforced the messages she was given as a child. However, after working with a therapist for a while, she was able to take control of her own life. Thereafter, she went to college and got a degree. From this point, she was able to make choices for herself and build some independent financial security. In terms of her process, she had got to the point where she couldn't hold the contradiction and move forward in her life. By working with a therapist, by looking at things through a different lens, she could see that her personality was being eclipsed and that her potential was being stifled. Once this realisation had occurred, it was impossible for her to hold herself back and she broke out of the dependency on her husband and took matters into her own hands. And, the way she saw the world and made sense of it, changed. It was not a massive change, it was just 'I can do this for myself' and with that, came a release of power and potential that carried her into a new life.

Waking up may also be triggered by something like being reacquainted with a significant (not necessarily pleasant) person. This may or may not be the person that wielded abuse but he or she may reignite the memory and call it back into being.

Claire's abusive carer was her grandfather and she placed a great deal of the blame for this on her mother. Firstly, it was her mother's father that abused her and secondly, her mother had done nothing to stop the abuse in spite of Claire's conviction that she knew what was going on. This may have been true on one level, but sometimes the unthinkable is so unthinkable that we don't give it conscious space in our minds. When this happens, it can look like collusion when actually it's more like self-protective denial. If Claire's mother had recognised and admitted what was going on, it would have required an intervention that would have rocked the foundation of her own life as well as the foundation of the family. Anyway, Claire interpreted her mother's apparent unwillingness to protect her as complicity and withdrew from her in silent anger. From her perspective, the relationship she had with her mother deteriorated so much that she found it hard to be in the same room as her. When, eventually, her mother went to live in America, Claire enjoyed the distance and made no contact with her for many years, until she returned one day without prior warning.

'I remember her standing in the kitchen, innocently giving me news about my grandfather, and my head just went 'bang'. That was one of the things that used to happen, my head would literally go bang inside. She was definitely one of the triggers for my process because once my head went 'bang', and she could see my reaction to her news, it all came out. Of course, she tried to deny all knowledge to begin with, but eventually it just tumbled out that she had known. She'd had the same thing happen to her as a child and she said that although she knew what was happening, she couldn't do anything about it. This was important to me because when there was no longer any doubt about my memories, when they had been recognised and verified, I was able to start doing something about my life because if I didn't, it would just continue to fall apart.'

In conversation with the women, I found that there were two kinds of trigger, one was cumulative and comprised a succession of small incremental steps that eventually built to a critical point of realisation; the other was a sudden and profound insight or experience that triggered the process. Claire's account is an example of the sudden realisation; although there was a great deal going on below the surface before her head went 'bang'. To add another layer of complexity, Claire's father had left at the height of her most vulnerable time and she always thought that he would return, like a knight in shining armour, to rescue her from her experiences. However, this didn't happen. He stayed away and eventually, after 35 years, Claire hired a private detective and found him. She arranged to go to see him and within half an hour of their first encounter for years, he said to her "It did stop, didn't it? I did everything I could to stop it!" As he said this, again she experienced a sudden physical sensation and she immediately felt validated and healed. Claire had described the legacy of her childhood experiences as a 'jagged river running through her' and, within moments of her father's acknowledgement, she said that she felt healed and that the river began to flow smoothly.

Initially, Claire thought of her father as someone who had abandoned her. This view was kept alive by the enduring disappointment that she felt during the years that he was absent from her life and the fact that he didn't come to rescue her. When he said that he had tried everything he could to stop the abuse, suddenly, her take on the situation was thrown into a different light and it brought about a dramatic change in perspective. This allowed her to broaden her view and accommodate the dichotomy – 'my father should love and protect me and be my hero' and 'my father abandoned me and left me vulnerable'. Both became true in Claire's eyes after she had met and spoken to him because she recognised that in abandoning her, her father had loved her and had hoped that the abuse would stop by virtue of his departure and, in this new light, it was a heroic act.

Having a fantasy about being rescued was a theme that was discussed by several of the women. When you are at your most vulnerable and when you are completely powerless to help yourself, the only place to go is into a fantasy where someone will take responsibility for what's happening to you and take you away from it all. Sometimes these fantasies would be about ending up in hospital so that people would *have* to take notice and do something; sometimes it was about being rescued by a Prince or Hero and sometimes it was about something dreadful happening to the abuser. Whichever path the fantasy took, it seeded an imaginative world were scenarios were built and stories invented to make the unbearable, bearable. It was another survival strategy.

Rachel had been given away by her mother as a young child of seven years. Rachel's mother had two daughters, one less robust and capable than the other. In her own abandonment, Rachel's mother felt she couldn't cope with both of her children so, believing that Rachel would cope better than her sister, she put Rachel into care. She justified this to herself by thinking that Rachel would get a better chance in life and more opportunity to succeed and survive. However, Rachel was sexually abused by the authority figures in whose care she was placed; her schooling was unsuccessful and she emerged without qualifications into adulthood feeling unloved, unwanted and unsuccessful. Rachel came to believe that the only way she could make sense of her life was to see it through religious eyes. At this point she turned to God, a kind person in her terms who accepted her in spite of her 'unwantability'.

In communion with God, Rachel felt accepted and loved. She was able to say anything to him and still be cared for; an experience that she didn't have in any other sphere of her life. She believed that this was the beginning of her becoming emotionally healthy because she could, at last, conceive of being lovable. Rachel went on to complete her schooling as a mature student and, to her surprise, found that she had capabilities and skills that she hadn't been aware of previously. Having learned to articulate and write down her thoughts and arguments, she went on to get a

Masters degree. She described her growing facility with language as an explosion that grew as she engaged with other intelligent people and was not only understood but her opinions were sought. This was incredibly empowering for her. At last, she could see herself through a different lens. She was no longer a useless, unwantable, unlovable being, in her terms, but an intelligent, articulate woman who could understand, learn and develop. She said: "Realising I wasn't stupid after all was amazingly liberating for me."

Rachel talks about one of her triggers; a profound and sudden moment of realisation in her healing journey. After the failure of her marriage, she decided to train to be a teacher so that she could stand on her own two feet and not be dependent on her former husband or on state welfare handouts.

'I thought I'd be a teacher. Actually, I gave myself two choices, teacher or priest. Why should I pick them? God knows, because both were places where I had been abused! Anyway they wouldn't have me as a priest because it wasn't allowed at the time, so I thought I'd go for teaching. It was a long and hard training and I eventually succeeded in becoming a teacher but what was important was the moment I stood in front of my first class as a fully paid up member of the teaching profession. Then I knew. I knew it wasn't my fault. I knew because seeing those kids there, doing what I told them, sitting there like neat little... I knew. And that's why I had to train as a teacher. I remember as clear as day. I stood up... and it wasn't when I was doing my practise but it was the moment I went to my first job, on my first day, and I remember what they talked about in assembly, that a journey of a thousand miles begins with a first step. That's why I had to do it. I stood up there, taking the register, thinking 'It wasn't my fault. It wasn't. It couldn't have been. How could it have been my fault at that age?' When you say to a kid, do this and do that and you don't take no for an answer, they've got to do it. So I knew.'

It is curious that many times, the women indicated that they felt that they had been put in the way of events that would assist in their understanding and healing. Perhaps they were guided by their own inner wisdom or perhaps the process itself had wisdom and orchestrated their experiences to take them to a certain point of understanding. Alternatively, it may be true that events constantly offer themselves as triggers and it is only when we are ready that we notice them. However, this is the key, unless you are 'conscious' or sufficiently aware, you won't notice them.

The frequency with which synchronous events happen is remarkable though. An unbelievable juxtaposition of events or circumstances. Extraordinary timings and coincidences. Just the right people arriving in your vicinity at just the right time and so on. It is as if these things are orchestrated purposefully, from some higher perspective, so that new light is cast on one disabling belief after another or so that a particular question is answered or need is met. And, as this happens, the power of the disabling belief or dysfunctional behaviour is slowly diminished until you are free to move on. All the women recounted journeys that were peppered with such phenomena; trigger points that ensured forward momentum was maintained even if it felt like a reversal in direction at times.

Saving graces: Waking up

'It is necessity and not pleasure that compels us.'
Dante's Inferno (Canto XII, 87)

The trigger creates a momentary insight that both illuminates the path and invites you to embark on the transformative journey. Once the trigger has been recognised, it cannot be un-recognised. To deny the trigger is as futile as trying to return toothpaste to the tube once it has been squeezed out. We may clasp our hands over our ears and shout loudly at the intrusion but we know intuitively that we can never again rest in our ignorance. Sometimes the trigger comes suddenly and unexpectedly whilst at other times it creeps up on us with subtlety and guile. Whatever its style, in reality, it is undisputed and we cannot ignore its injunction to take the first steps to change.

Fear of the unknown often prevents us from taking the first transformative steps however. Most of us fear that we will fall into the abyss or even be annihilated, but this fear does not preserve us or serve us well. It literally petrifies us and renders us unable to utilise our full potential. If we succumb to fear, we will live a 'half-life' only, never knowing the joy of our innate creative expression or the wonder of being free to choose. The rewards of overcoming fear are great but these, seemingly, are not incentives enough to encourage us in our moment of choice. Instead, they remain abstract concepts that apply so obviously to others but not to us. People just don't understand the uniqueness and extremity of our own situation!

Terms such as shock and devastation have been used to describe the feelings that erupt after a trigger has been experienced. These are dramatic words that carry physical, mental and emotional symptoms. Your body may start shaking uncontrollably or your heart may thump in your chest. You may sweat, feel sick, or faint. As well, you may feel great sadness, hopelessness, isolation or despair whilst your mind attempts to 'make sense' of what caused these reactions. Happily, positive triggers also exist that release high levels of physical energy and bring feelings of happiness and joy, but these are less likely to be experienced at the outset of the transformative journey of healing, rather, they are held as promises to be experienced along the way.

Breath

One of the saving graces in moments of high tension is the breath. Mostly, we breathe without thinking, allowing our bodies to regulate our breath in a way that delivers sufficient oxygen to the blood to sustain life and to fuel our bodies in action. However, when we are shocked and carried away by events, the steady rhythm of our breath is also carried away. When this happens, we either stop breathing altogether (the freeze response) or we take quick, deep breaths from the top of our lungs (the fight or flight response). In the first instance, the lack of breathing allows us to be stock still and provoke no further danger whilst our body sorts and sends the appropriate signals to the nervous system and/or whilst we think about what to do. In extremis, however, the lack of breath deprives our blood of oxygen and this can lead to a blackout.

In the second instance, the rapid breathing super-charges the blood with oxygen which prepares us for the 'fight' or 'flight' response. However, if we neither fight nor take flight our rapid breathing can lead to hyperventilation. Hyperventilation is caused by a reduction of carbon dioxide in the blood (because we are breathing it out all the time) which constricts the arteries. This reduces the flow of blood to the muscles and ends up depriving the body of oxygen. Hyperventilation results in a feeling of being out of breath which then stimulates over-breathing. The more we breathe, the less oxygen is at our disposal (because the arteries are constricted); and the less oxygen we have at our disposal, the more we breathe. Hyperventilation leads to a rapid pulse, a dry mouth and a tightness around the chest area. In extreme cases, a tingling or fizzing sensation is experienced in the fingertips, lips and other extremities. This can be alleviated by cupping our hands over the nose and mouth and breathing in oxygen depleted and carbon dioxide enriched air. However, it is hoped that this remedy isn't commonly required for most people.

When the breath is carried away by stressful circumstances, a reversal of control is helpful. Breathing consciously and deliberately to establish a slower rhythm will reduce some of the symptoms and help your body return to its normal function. We often hear people advise someone in shock to 'take a deep breath' or 'breathe deeply and slowly'. Instinctively, we know that this will alleviate some of the physical symptoms of shock.

There are many techniques that help you master your breath. Yoga is an obvious and good technique for mastering breathing. It brings consciousness to the breath; a helpful commodity in anyone's language!

Physical contact and warmth

Another saving grace is physical contact and warmth. If you are alone, this could be a blanket wrapped around you and drawn up to your neck as you process your experience. Sometimes, climbing into bed and pulling the duvet close is comforting, a hot bath or a cup of tea may be helpful. If there is someone present that you trust (an important condition), you may find an arm around you makes you feel calmer and safer until the initial shock has worn off. However, the physical side of shock is not all there is. Emotionally, you may need to be assured that you are not alone in your troubles; that someone is with you, supporting and caring for you. Even if you don't want to get close to someone, it is often helpful merely to share space with another human being or animal. Sitting together, breathing together, can be all that is needed.

Find someone to talk to

As time distances you from your trigger, other requirements come into play. Sometimes these are practicalities, other times these requirements may be something like having someone to talk to so that you can empty your mind of the experience. Clear or create sufficient physical space so that you can sit down calmly and comfortably and allow your mind to digest what has happened. It is important to meet your immediate needs without entering a state of denial where you convince yourself that nothing has really changed. Metaphorically speaking, denial makes it possible to continue walking whilst dragging a broken leg behind you. It doesn't matter what the event is that triggers your process, if you deny it, you can be sure that it will be more dramatic next time. So don't put off the hour of your awakening. Take heed of the title of a well-known book by Susan Jeffers: *Feel the fear and do it anyway!*

Tap into your natural strength

Perhaps the most important saving grace at this stage of the process is the fact that in times of crisis, most people find great and previously untapped strength. It seems that the human fibre strengthens in moments of greatest need. There are many examples of physical strength being magnified at times of crisis when the 'fight' or 'flight' response is stimulated. However, it is not just within the physical body that strength manifests, the emotional and mental bodies strengthen too. People 'hold themselves together' frequently in situations that are potentially unravelling. 'Staying strong' for a needy partner or child, 'saving the tears until later' when being given a bad piece of news, or 'putting oneself second' are not uncommon reactions in severely stressful or shocking situations. Even when people claim that they are 'falling apart', there is an opposite force holding them together which outweighs the sense of collapse they may be feeling. On reflection, people often remark that they don't know where they got their strength from or what resources they were using to get through a crisis. These are instances of saving graces that come to the rescue when they are needed most and they can be relied upon to carry you through whatever shock or devastation you happen to be experiencing.

STAGE 1 - CONNECTING: THE BEGINNING OF THE DESCENT

She left the web: she left the loom:
She made three paces thro' the room:
She saw the waterflower bloom:
She saw the helmet and the plume:
She looked down to Camelot.

Out flew the web, and floated wide,
The mirror cracked from side to side,
"The curse is come upon me," cried
The Lady of Shallot.

The Lady of Shallot, Ed Org   **Alfred, Lord Tennyson – 1809-1892**

I have reversed this image of The Lady of Shallot to indicate that she no longer looks at life reflected in the mirror but has turned to see the scene through her window directly. In the poem, the curse leads to her death, a seemingly negative reward for getting to grips with reality. However, after every death comes a birth so I like to see this as the end of living out of consciousness and the beginning of living in consciousness.

This phase is often characterised by a feeling of standing on the edge of the abyss and looking in, knowing that it holds trials and challenges that will scorch and burn. The 'Oh my God!' dread that comes with it and the inevitability of the descent into chaos floods the woman, who might consider walking away, back to the territory where her dysfunctional behaviours will enable her to continue living a half-life. To jump over the edge means that it is no longer possible to hide behind ignorance of the coping strategies which, by the way, are failing rapidly. Not to jump spells collusion; an unacceptable behaviour for any conscious, choosing adult. Dammed if you do; dammed if you don't! In the cold light of scrutiny, someone choosing not to jump will know that they are deliberately fighting their way back into their dysfunction. Yet still, there is an enormous temptation to turn and walk away as realisation of the extent of the journey dawns. However, by turning, you would only be flying in the face of the laws of the universe in the vain hope that they will not prevail and that somehow, it is possible to 'un-know' the truth of your own insight.

Desperation and rising panic may be the tenor of the experience as you feel both the resistance and the compulsion to jump. However, this must be weighed against the inescapable, for not to jump will leave you ricocheting from realisation to denial at increasing speed and severity until you are returned again to the point of choice. This is the way of the process.

Yet the structure of society conspires to keep people, especially women, in their victim-consciousness when faced with a dilemma of life-transforming proportions. It is more convenient that way and many institutions play their part in maintaining the status quo. At such moments, the medical profession has a tendency to over-administer mind-calming drugs in the hope that the needy patients will disappear from their professional radar screens. In addition, although we are seeing some relaxation in the mindsets of doctors, alternative and complementary approaches are viewed with suspicion or cynicism. Naturally, this leads to patients being discouraged from managing their own healing process.

It seems that the education system also serves to keep initiative and enterprise at bay and prevents youngsters from entering the life-fray where they can test their edges. Schools and Colleges spoon-feed acceptable thinking patterns and consider those who conform to be good students. There is little room for building life skills or for exploring the inner landscape where personal richness may be found. For those with different intelligences such as art, music, dance and drama, a battle lies ahead as they struggle to prove their worth in a 'winner takes all' adult world.

The media too seems to enjoy romanticising the victim.

As I write, I am reminded of a phenomenon named 'woundology' by Caroline Myss[2]. She proposes that, in these days of 'therapeutic fluency', a new intimate language has developed that legitimises the revelation of wounds as a means of binding relationships. Indeed, this has become such common practice that it could be seen as the 'currency' of relationships, a currency which is used to control situations and people, both inside and outside the therapeutic environment. We see this phenomenon enacted on television chat shows which dig deep into the intimate lives of volunteers and sensationalise wounds that in previous eras would have been considered shaming and kept secret for the sake of social nicety. Exchanging dramatic stories and entering the one-upmanship game for the purposes of 'good television' does nothing to release potential or personal truth. It merely perpetuates the negative cycle that keeps us stuck in the past and prevents us from thriving and being happy.

Taking personal responsibility and control it seems, is counter to our social norms, even though this is espoused and apparently encouraged in political rhetoric. But it is exactly these human qualities that are required if personal transformation is going to be achieved and if society is going to evolve in the long-term. Whatever the severity of your past history, if you are to release yourself, you must take responsibility for the choices you make and the control you have over your life. If you are to find personal reward and happiness, it is at this stage of the process, where past coping strategies are starkly identified and fear has peaked, that your choice is there to be made.

It makes it all the more remarkable that the women who presented their account of this critical stage of the process did so reflectively and without fanfare. Perhaps their courage stemmed from the fact that the full impact of their choice was not obvious when they made it; a common feature of many life-changing choices such as marriage, becoming a parent or choosing a career. It was only in retrospect, when the effects of their dedication to self-improvement and the emotional buffeting they had received had passed, that they were able to look back objectively and articulate the process that they had followed. In this way, and in this spirit, they were able to identify the coping strategies that they had employed in order to maintain some semblance of normality in their lives.

The themes of 'living on two levels', 'compartmentalising', 'undertaking displacement activities' and 'disassociating' were common strategies that protected the women from facing their pain. Others included rather more obsessive/addictive behaviours such as self-harming, eating disorders, workaholism, alcoholism and drug abuse. Once the process had been triggered though, the women had to reveal to themselves the truth of their coping behaviours. They also had to acknowledge the fact that they would not be served by perpetuating them.

Heather talked about her revelation that the coping strategies she had employed in the past were no longer working. This stage preceded the next stage of disintegrating only by a short distance but it was distinctive nevertheless and many get stuck here. At this point, like many, Heather could have tried to claw it all back together again and hurriedly invent another strategy that would prevent her from facing the truth of her dysfunctional life. But having done this several times already, this would have been a bridge too far. This time, the choice didn't really exist. For her and the other women, it was clear that once the realisation had been made; in spite of a flurry of attempts to drown it out, it was too late.

A new relationship, undertaking an educational programme or signing up for a training course are often used as displacement activities at this time. They are designed to hold things in check but these strategies are ultimately ineffective. The slide has begun and there is no going back. This stage has the tone of someone clinging on to the edge of a cliff whilst their fingertips are being prised away forcefully.

We have identified the 'same age' trigger and, indeed, Heather's revelation occurred when her daughter reached the same age that she had been when she first experienced abuse by her father. At this point, she started to withdraw from her nurturing role as a mother and found that she could no longer give her children the kind of physical contact and affection they needed. Although things were ticking over, the cracks were beginning to show and she recognised that her children, and other observers, were beginning to notice her obsessive compulsive behaviours and had gently started questioning her about them.

Looking back, Heather managed to link her coping strategies to her past experiences and describe the connections between them. By doing this, she was able to recognise the tactics she had developed that enabled her to keep going. She also recognised that these tactics were able to override what she was feeling on the inside; they masked her truth.

As Heather was reflecting on her past and relaying her experiences to me she was actually joining the dots, so to speak, and making connections between events in her past. Our conversation enabled her to bring to light her past experience, examine the effect it had had on her life, and identify the coping strategies that she had invented to keep the lid on things. Casting her mind back from the safety of a new vantage point, Heather could see the tendency she had to compartmentalise her life; to live on several levels at the same time. She saw that she reserved one set of behaviours for one role or situation, and a different set of behaviours for another. In doing this, she was able to disassociate from her childhood experiences and keep them out of her conscious mind. However, although the wall that she'd built around herself succeeded in protecting her from facing the challenges and pain of her past, it also succeeded in anaesthetising her from life's experiences – including parenting her children.

With the help of a longer perspective, Heather realised that there was a bit of her that never came out and, in order to protect this most vulnerable part of herself, she put on roles which she played so convincingly that no-one questioned her about them; not even her. Each of her faces was being carefully composed to portray a particular image and, in this way, Heather was able to protect herself from being revealed. Sustaining this kind of strategy is only possible if the energy required to do so is equal in measure to the desire to deny personal truth. In Heather's case, all the emotional muscle at her disposal was working hard to ensure that each of her faces was managed properly and presented consistently. Eventually, the tension was so great that it became almost impossible to keep the multitude of faces in play. Now she was in real danger of being unmasked and revealed, and somewhere inside she 'knew' this. Yet she still sought protection and, in a final attempt to avoid the threat to her being, Heather invented still more faces and took on still more roles. Indeed, in her attempt to avoid her worst fears, she said, her faces were multiplying all over the place. Keeping the house meticulously clean was one of the roles she adopted obsessively to compensate for others that were under threat of coming undone – until, that is, she was so exhausted, physically, emotionally and spiritually, that she had to let it all go and begin her journey in earnest.

I'm sharing this part of Heather's journey because she articulated so well the dilemma she felt at embarking on something that she intuitively knew would be challenging and difficult. I'm sure you've heard people making up all sorts of reasons why they shouldn't do something that will disturb their status quo. "I can't start a training programme while the children are young.", "I'm too old to learn anything new!", "I have an obligation... a duty....I promised....it wouldn't be fair to my family.....!!!! I write these fluidly because I have used them all. So often, it seems, as I stare into the abyss with apparent choice, I find a talent for listing the reasons why it is not the moment to jump! Have you heard yourself say these things too?

Saving graces: Connecting

'I do not want the peace that passeth understanding. I want the understanding which bringeth peace.'
Helen Keller

Of course, as human beings, we all need coping strategies. They provide the social oil that allows us to fit into different situations confidently. It is just when these strategies eclipse our inner being through overuse that they become a problem. This is the ultimate 'hide and seek'. We literally hide from ourselves when our strategies define the person we are seen to be and, as a result, we end up losing our ability to access our inner knowing. If we construct a mask and use it to define us, rather than letting who we are define the face we present to the world, we create a vast distance between our true self and the self that others see. Yet those others respond to us according to what we put out, so they will trust that our mask is us and respond to us accordingly. This is fine when we are conscious and in control of our different faces but if we are not, we can find ourselves in situations that are not natural to us and for which we are not equipped to cope. For instance, if we put on a mask of social confidence, we may be summonsed to display this in circumstances where we are at our most vulnerable. Perhaps this would be at a party where we might wish to maintain our social boundaries and prevent too much intimacy.

Although you may recognise that you have employed protective coping strategies throughout your life, you may find it difficult to pin down exactly what these are and wonder how you managed to put them into practice without apparent awareness or choice. Trying to make sense of your coping strategies may seem a bit daunting at first. You may begin by looking at your circumstances and have a general disliking for what you see. You may also look at where you've been and dislike what you have experienced. Perhaps you will forlornly ask yourself what guarantee there is for the future.

To balance the gloom of these observations, reflect on those areas in your life where you are confident and successful. There are bound to be many. Just as our strengths can be weaknesses, so our perceived weaknesses can be strengths. If you look at the landscape of your life objectively you will be compelled to recognise that you have not been utterly defeated nor have you totally lost your reasoning powers or innate capabilities. In fact, your coping has made you strong in a way that many people are denied, and it may have been responsible for bringing you to a valuable turning point which will carry you through the remainder of your life in a happy and rewarding way. So a moment of appreciation of your inventiveness and guile in creating such robust mechanisms may put a little substance beneath your feet and act as a saving grace as you move forward.

Identify the patterns
The 'Pacifier' - If you are having difficulty identifying your coping strategies, look at your past relationships. Relationships, if you care to look at them truthfully, are where we see ourselves reflected in all our ugliness and glory! There is no escape from our self in relationship. Try listing out the reasons for your past relationship failures and look for the patterns (or payoffs) that underlie them all. You may recall yourself saying to close friends "I always seem to end up with men who think they know what's best for me!" If this is the sort of thing you've heard yourself saying, you may have inadvertently entered a series of relationships where you unconsciously thought that if you do as he asks; he'll love you and take care of you. This unhealthy exchange of favours binds 'obedience' to 'love' and diminishes, or completely denies, your own needs. Your coping strategy may have been that of 'pleaser' or 'pacifier' and it has the payoff of making you feel acceptable to another, when you may not feel acceptable to yourself. This reluctance to take responsibility is, perhaps, a relic from the past when you were forced to obey others'

commands in exchange for 'life support'; when you had to 'earn' your own sustenance because you were not made to feel worthy of it by virtue of your existence alone.

The 'Rescuer' - Another example is the statement: "I can't imagine why I didn't see it coming. He actually *told* me that he was a heavy drinker when we first met. I might have known he was an alcoholic!" Although it may seem strange, being needed by another person brings a payoff of security and (relative) stability. However, it also creates a mutually dependent relationship that is only sustainable as long as the mutual benefits of the dependency remain in place. By putting yourself in service to another, your life and relationship is given purpose and, in exchange for the service, you will be loved and appreciated back (or at least needed). And, in exchange for the love and appreciation (or neediness) you will continue to serve. This dysfunctional dynamic can only exist for as long as you are prepared to be distracted from thinking about yourself and your own needs. In this case, the coping strategy may be 'rescuer' or 'helper'.

The rescuer is very much my pattern and, at a recent workshop, I was encouraged to write a poem about the lure of being a rescuer. This is what I wrote:

In my pursuit of purpose, I hang on to the needs of others
like a life-raft that carries me into the dark waters of my own fears.

As I look back, the mud-sucking pull slowly reveals
the arrogance of rescue and the fear of my own truth.

A hand grips my head and turns it, as if on a screw thread.
I am compelled to look into the murk.

My eyes take a while to adjust. I can no longer return.

This is the awakening. This is my resignation.

In the inevitability of the journey to the inner landscape
I am cracked and broken.

I release. I release. I release!

The 'Provocateur' - Here's another: "I thought he was different but again, I seemed to have found a jealous guy!" When a possessive lover fears humiliation or loss, whether there's good reason for it or not, anger and the need to exercise control rise to the surface and tend to get expressed in an aggressive and accusatory way. If these fears of loss are managed well and expressed calmly and honestly, positive feelings of being precious and being loved may emerge. However, when they are held at an unhealthy level, they become undermining and destructive. The dysfunctional linkage is 'love expressed as anger'. For instance, your unconscious message may be 'If he didn't love me so much, he wouldn't get so angry!' or 'If he didn't need me so much, he wouldn't be so terrified of losing me.' The *perceived* game is that of 'provocateur' and, if used deliberately, can result in the most dramatic sense of being 'seen' and 'feeling important'. Often the drama results in equally energetic sexual reconciliations, which brings the payoff of feeling sexually powerful. It can, of course, result in physical violence, returning the recipient to the victim role.

The 'Victim' - The position of 'victim' can be a very powerful one and bring its own illusion of control, in childhood as well as in adulthood. Sharon spoke of her position as the abused child being quite a powerful one.

'People who have been abused have quite a lot of power. No, perhaps I should say that *I* felt that I was quite powerful. However bad the situation is, you think you're controlling it and so to give up your power is quite a big thing. Of course, I can only say it from my perspective but I had thought I was controlling the world by keeping quiet. My grandfather was a very nasty man who told me that we'd all end up in care if I told anyone, so while it was all going on, I was keeping everybody together; that was my creation. Everybody was all right. The boys were still going to school. Mum and Dad were OK. I could handle it if it meant that the family stayed together, so I felt quite omnipotent. Everybody was all right and *I'd* made sure that everybody was all right. That was quite a powerful place to be. I think it's a shock then, when you lose control by telling someone. I felt I lost control of the situation that I was in even though it was completely out of my control! It's all messed up, isn't it, but part of the thought process for me was, 'I'm not in charge of this any more.' While it was going on, and while nobody knew, I could handle it. When you give that power away by telling somebody, you've lost a lot of control.'

In this passage, Sharon has managed to present the complex issue of the 'powerful victim'; a seeming contradiction in terms. No one other than an abused child could have expressed this as she did.

Claim the pattern that's yours

'Playing the victim', however distasteful a concept, is not an uncommon way of wounded adults finding a sense of security or power. Of course, there are extremely complex undertows and many different ways of looking at these situations. This is why no one can *really* interpret your patterns for you. Only you can know the truth about how they evolved and what the intricacies of them are designed to achieve. Looking at your patterns demands that you let go of all the preconceptions you have of yourself and that you look with seeing eyes and cutting honesty at the evidence and repercussions of your strategies.

You may not have got what you wanted by exercising your strategies because they are likely to have been based on a distorted premise. Yet in your commitment to them, and in your commitment to reaching your desired objective, you probably kept on employing them, over and over again. You may even have amplified your strategies when they did not work the first time, believing that if you tried harder, somehow your objectives would more likely to be met. 'If at first you don't succeed...' and all that. You may also be amazed that you didn't grasp the fact that your strategies were ineffective sooner and try something different. But it's easy to have wisdom after the event and nothing is as obvious or as simple as it seems in hindsight. Merely noticing your patterns is a helpful start when you are considering your own path. Try not to judge them or be harsh on yourself. Just take the information that they are offering you and use it to inform the next steps of your journey.

For many of the women I spoke to, their habitual coping strategies created and perpetuated the need to protect and defend themselves. As adults, they inevitably attracted relationships that struck the familiar chords of childhood, which meant that surrender to an intimate partner was emotionally or physically too dangerous to contemplate. However, to find themselves, these women needed to build relationships that reflected their truth, not those that reinforced their dysfunction. To be vulnerable to a friend or partner and to receive oneself in their reflection is vital for advancement and growth. For this group of women, their inability to yield to another and to be vulnerable was something they had learned and perfected as children and, as adults; they didn't have the understanding or the inclination to change their responses. Indeed, the tried and tested coping strategies remained necessary because they were fishing for intimacy in a dysfunctional pool and drawing relationships to them that echoed those they experienced in the past. However, as these behaviours increasingly distanced themselves from the truth of their core being, the situation gradually became intolerable until it reached a critical point. It was almost as if an inner trip-switch was thrown when the denial of the Self became too great. At this point, there was no option but to look into the darkness of their own reflection. To ignore the impetus to do this would only further increase the pain and further distance them from their truth. There was little choice but to listen to the voice that came from within and remain sensitive to its wisdom as it guided them through their transformation.

Often, potential partners recognise our coping strategies at a subliminal level and, if they happen to accord with their own, they act as attractors that draw us to them in a complex dance which is defined by a tacit agreement of dysfunctional co-operation. In this way, one set of behaviours reinforces the other and a history of abuse turns into a promise of more as the opposing patterns weave together and work themselves out in perpetual motion. The victim remains the victim, putting out subtle victim messages until a random perpetrator picks them up and enters the familiar territory where abuse is the currency of communication on the physical, emotional, sexual, psychological and/or spiritual dimension. This dynamic is so familiar to each party that neither knows it, nor can they do anything about it, until one or other of them experiences the trigger that wakes them up to the unacceptability of the situation. Whilst the dysfunction exists and serves its purpose, it is experienced as confirmatory and familiar. The people in this relationship may think 'This is the order of things', 'This is how it always is', 'All is well in the world'.

Even when the inappropriateness of a coping strategy is recognised, it is not always easy to change it. Firstly, it can mean the termination of an established relationship or set of relationships with far reaching consequences and secondly, these behaviours have been established for many years for good reasons and it is not always easy, or wise, to discard them completely. So, even when they are unnecessary, the strategies remain in place, habitually playing themselves out to colluding audiences. So, rather than reaching for a radical change, what we can achieve by looking incisively at our coping strategies, is a change in our awareness. Once the patterns have been recognised and observed both dispassionately and compassionately, we can place our attention on them and observe them in action. With this conscious observation, we get the opportunity to re-write them. This is the beginning of transformation and change.

Identify a range of new behaviours

If you find yourself engaging in a coping strategy that you wish to change or discard, try not to get frustrated. Look back on the situation or incident and ask yourself, or a trusted friend, what you could have done differently. You need to learn to be discerning about what you do and don't do to protect yourself. Some aspects of your coping strategies will be valuable to keep so don't necessarily discard them in their entirety; you may want to import some of the old behaviours into your new way of being.

Find yourself a role model, someone who you've observed managing difficult situations and who you admire for their ability to do so. You can practice using some of their behaviours to see how they feel to you but put them to use in safe settings where the outcome is not critical. This is one way of deciding whether or not they feel natural to you and whether you wish to adopt them permanently. Not all will feel right but some may enter your behavioural toolkit easily and effectively. This is not about becoming something you're not, rather it's about extending the authenticity of who you are through new behaviours that reflect your inner truth and sense of Self.

Find the 'payoff' in your dysfunctional relationships

If your coping strategies are being perpetuated unchecked, they could have nasty consequences for you and for the quality of your life. As is so often the case, the knowledge, attributes and behaviours that have got us to where we are today are not the same as those that will carry us into the future. This is the essence of learning and growth. It brought us from our childhood view of the world and it will take us into our adulthood. Just as a plant or a tree sheds its leaves in the winter to make room for new growth in the spring, we must shed our redundant views and behaviours to make way for new growth as we circle through the seasons of our lives. Letting go is of paramount importance in this progressive movement. Hanging on merely blocks your path and restricts your potential. Indeed, in your contraction against new ways of thinking and acting, you become stagnant as a human being and behaviourally in-grown, like a toenail with nowhere else to grow but back on itself, unhealthily and painfully.

Some of the women experienced the worst excesses of their coping strategies in their adult years. Even though these had once served their needs, they had become destructive as they inveigled their way into the adult context. Like continuing to swat at a fly that has gone, these coping strategies continued to define a set of responses in spite of the necessity for them having disappeared. In some instances, it was this excess that triggered the process of transformation.

Whatever your coping strategies are, they will have been created by you in response to a particular situation. They will be complex and convoluted so don't worry if you can't decipher them straight away. You may need to enter a protracted period of self-observation and dwell on your behaviour over some time, but remember, asking for feedback and being open to what is reflected to you by those who know you well is a good way in. It is amazing how objective and opinionated people can be if you give them half a chance – but do put conditions around their feedback. Reserve the right to reject it if it doesn't strike you as helpful.

STAGE 2 - DISINTEGRATING: THE FALL INTO DESPAIR

Turning and turning in the widening gyre
The falcon cannot hear the falconer;
Things fall apart; the centre cannot hold;
Mere anarchy is loosed upon the world,
The blood-dimmed tide is loosed, and everywhere
The ceremony of innocence is drowned;
The best lack all convictions, while the worst
Are full of passionate intensity.

Pandora's Box, Ed Org

The Second Coming - W. B. Yeats

There are several different legends about Pandora, but they seem to agree that she was made by the Gods to punish mankind. Each God endowed her with a special quality to make her attractive, other than Zeus, who, in his anger, gave her the qualities of foolishness and mischievousness. Although she had been cautioned not to open a box in the house of her lover, Epimetheus, her curiosity got the better of her and she opened it, only to let free the scourges of disease, sorrow, poverty and crime. In her horror, she slammed the lid closed, incarcerating Hope, whose mission was to heal the suffering caused by the scourges. Eventually Pandora opened the box a second time to release Hope. This picture is appropriate to accompany this stage of the transformative process as it couples despair with hope.

Emma, who came from a family where the physical and sexual boundaries were breached, connected with the image of Pandora's Box not only as a metaphor for her life but also when she talked about the disintegrating phase of her process and her subsequent fall into despair:

'I had a real lifelong fear of being a bit of a Pandora's Box; that nobody knew what they were getting into if they started opening things up with me. This was rooted in the maternal messages I received about being 'bad', 'evil' and 'wicked' which I knew in my mind were totally irrational but could never get rid of. Anyway, these messages kept me from sharing myself with somebody else. I just had this fear that I would overwhelm them with all the things in my 'box' if I let them witness me opening up and then they wouldn't be available to support me any more. Then, it would be like nobody would be 'anchored' and they would be adrift with me in all the chaos.'

Feelings of spiralling out of control, fragmentation, falling into a black hole, depression and despair are common themes amongst all models of transformation. Transformation demands that we let go of something so that we are free to build something new. As we enter the process, this letting go relates to our current personality, or aspects of our current personality; those aspects that have begun to fail us as we grow in maturity. The personality is experienced by others through our characteristic patterns of behaviour; through our purposeful activity and through our responses to circumstances and situations. These facets of our personalities have been built and conditioned in the formative years of our lives and have become habitual through repetitive use. They compose and characterise the person we are known as which draws others with similar traits. However, these features of our personality are not an intrinsic part of us; they are projections or distortions that emanate from our essence or core. They are the masks that we use to interface and engage with the world. It is by letting go of our investment in these emanations that we are able to find and release our core being. However, in the act of letting go, personal chaos ensues.

Perhaps it would be helpful to view the process in the same way as you might a trapeze artist in flight. The trapeze artist has to let go of one trapeze before being able to transfer to another. There is a short moment when she is suspended in space, no safety net, no going back. All that carries her forward is her intention and the momentum she has built up from increasing the arc of her swing. Bystanders may think her completely mad as they watch her let go at such a moment of vulnerability in order to test a belief that she will find something solid to grab on to as she flies through the air. It is the same dynamic when we let go of our old masks or personality traits. At the time when we have most invested in how we are perceived as mothers, partners, career women … we are driven to let go and become unprotected and vulnerable. At that moment, all we have is a belief in our Self and the momentum of our determination (which is not always conscious or willing!) to find that Self. Just as the trapeze artist cannot change her mind mid-flight, nor can we, not without falling. So we are left with a choice; instead of falling, we are given the option to let go with confidence and trust that, despite our greatest fears, we will be carried forward to find a new and secure place. Is this really a choice? I suppose it is better than choosing to land in an undignified heap on the ground. So, if you find yourself 'falling', perhaps it is as well to do so purposefully! I remember the scene in Toy Story when Buzz Lightyear is encouraged by his friend Woody to believe he is flying. To which he replies: "This isn't flying, it's falling – with style!"

Staying with the metaphor of the trapeze artist for a little longer, think of her as she carries herself from one bar to another. In performing this manoeuvre, she de-stabilises or unbalances herself, reorients her position and continues to swing on a different trajectory. In 'transformation-speak', this may be considered to be the movement away from an identification with one mask in order to create another; a half revolution as we change the direction we're facing, from a focus on the past to a focus on the future. As we leave behind who we were, we may recognise that all that we formerly held to be true is no longer so. These feelings can be accompanied by feelings of anxiety or even depression.

Heather talks of this stage in her process and illustrates most graphically the chaos that ensued when she was forced from the familiar territory of her personality and experienced the loss of control and the loss of her sense of Self.

'Things started to come undone. It was as if I'd been holding on very tightly to all these threads but now they were being pulled out of my hands and I just couldn't keep hold of them any more. Although I managed to function quite well on the surface, there was a bit of me that was always hidden, and that was the bit that was in danger of being exposed. Then my mother died and I just couldn't do it anymore. I couldn't keep up this pretence; although it wasn't a conscious pretence, and all these threads were just snapping out of my grasp and everything was coming undone. I'd been struggling along thinking that I would be able to do what I'd always done and hold it all together, but I couldn't. It was impossible. At the same time, all these other boxes were opening up. Everything was coming unhinged and all the behaviours that I had had before which enabled me to cope were no longer working. Nothing was working. In fact I couldn't get a hold of *anything*. I think everything was falling apart, disintegrating really, because my strategies for coping weren't working.'

Heather's account finds natural resonance with Yeats' words: 'Things fall apart; the centre cannot hold; Mere anarchy is loosed upon the world...' Heather: 'Things started to come undone; I just couldn't keep hold of them; Everything was falling apart, disintegrating.' Of course, it is no surprise that accounts of this natural human journey have found their way into myth, legend, poetry and literature, but when the words are so similar, it feels remarkable.

Other women's conversations about this part of their journey focused on a similar theme, although they used different words to describe how they felt about it. Sharon felt that she dropped into a black hole as she abandoned her work and moved away from her family. She had confronted her grandfather unsuccessfully and felt so despairing and angry that she couldn't think of any other way of dealing with it than to withdraw. Yet she also saw this time as very positive because in the privacy of her own environment, she was able to release the anger that she hadn't been able to reach before and prepare herself for the next leg of her journey. She called this a time of 'latent healing'; when subtle changes and adjustments were percolating through her consciousness and all she had to do was be aware of and respond to her feelings. She let go of the process and allowed it to guide her from this point on.

Others also suggested that when things fell apart, it was a time for release; a time when all the energy that was required to hold things together could be expressed as red-fire anger. This anger came out in different ways depending on the nature of the person expressing it. Some vented their anger physically, hacking at a cushion with a serrated kitchen knife. Some shouted, some screamed, some hurled things across a room. All cried a river.

Heather, so articulate in the way she described her experiences, tells of the way her anger emerged, and re-emerged:

'I cried a lot. I was angry. I was very angry. My Dad had died. He had this room that was his private space. He did all sorts of things in there, making stuff, mending things, hanging out. Well, we had to go in there and clear it out after he died. I had thought I wouldn't go into this room because this was where he used to take me when I was little. But I did. I felt almost drawn to it. I started to put things together in boxes until I found the box where he stored the things that he used for my abuse. And it started with that. I just smashed it. I thought I had dealt with all my anger over the years but I hadn't. It just pumped up inside me and I started smashing things. I smashed so many things in there! I was just furious really. I was so bloody angry. And I was upset. I smashed that room to smithereens and then I smashed it some more. I was exhausted afterwards, and then I sat and cried. And then I just left it because I couldn't do anything with it. My anger was the thing that I had a lot of trouble with. I couldn't get angry for a long time, but I was angry that day. Really angry that day.'

Sometimes anger is not expressed energetically like this, rather it is a slow seeping toxicity that permeates and sabotages relationships. Because it is not acknowledged and faced, it is inevitably expressed in passive-aggressive behaviours. These may be self-destructive or they may be observed or felt by others through snide quips or put-downs. Sadly, unexpressed anger seeds itself in the fabric of the body and can lead to physical symptoms of disease. It can also often be seen through the expressions or in the lines on people's faces as they age. I remember as a child, if I thought a hateful thought and pulled an ugly face, my mother would warn me that the wind might change and sentence me to a lifetime of ugliness! Perhaps there is ancient wisdom in this old wives' tale and that perpetual thought patterns really do create physical reality. Musing on this, I sometimes look at the faces of the elderly and speculate on their life path and the attitudes they held during it and, when I see an elderly but joyous face, I am reminded of the importance of resolving anger and attaining spiritual health and happiness.

Building on the emotional/physical link for a moment, some notable researchers have found that psychological ill health can certainly lead to physical symptoms and illness; sometimes chronic illness. Not only this, but the specific manifestation of disease can act as a diagnostic tool pointing towards the cause of the problem. Writers who have connected a negative psychological or emotional disposition to physical dysfunction and ill health include Caroline Myss, who co-wrote *The Creation of*

Health with her colleague Norman Shealy, and Louise Hay, who wrote *You Can Heal Your Life.* Both books argue the case for a causal link between certain diseases and their emotional or psychological counterparts. You might like to have a look at them as they may give you useful insights and help you reflect on your own psycho-physical linkages.

Saving graces: Disintegrating

"Come to the edge." he said.
They said, "We are afraid."
"Come to the edge." he said.
They came.
He pushed them... and they flew.
Guillaume Apollinaire

Although this stage of the process is often coupled with feelings of confusion and despair, its saving grace rests in the fact that it challenges the way you make sense of the world. As it does this, it also challenges your old and ineffective coping mechanisms. The blessing (and the curse!) of this stage is that once the guts of your meaning mesh have been spilled in the revelatory process, you can't un-spill them; it is irreversible. And, although, the option to return to former habits of thinking and behaving is taken from you, the opportunity to create a new set of responses is given to you. This happens because the unconscious channels along which your thoughts formerly travelled have been brought into consciousness; the way you made choices has been revealed. And, in truth, you now can't justify your old coping strategies. Indeed, you might be considered crazy to re-choose your past self-defeating reactions and responses in full consciousness. Now you are on the rollercoaster. You have travelled at speed into the trough, and there is nothing for it but to negotiate your way out of it using all the resources and support you can muster. It may perhaps be cold comfort but at least you are conscious now and you cannot return to unconsciousness without premeditated denial and collusion; two coping strategies that can only serve as temporary respites before they begin to sabotage your progress.

In the morass, your saving grace is consciousness and the conscious rebuilding of meaning. As you feel yourself slide into a chaotic place, it is easy to believe that everything, even your Self, has been swept away and there is nothing to hang on to. Sometimes this is accompanied by a physical sense of movement or a feeling that the ground is shifting under foot. You may also feel an adrenalin rush, a sense of foreboding, anxiety or fear.

Unbelievable though it may seem when you are encountering this phenomenon for the first time, you may find these emotions change to those of anticipation and excitement on successive occasions. However, at the outset (in consciousness), it is easy to catastrophise and build dramatic scenarios of emptiness and annihilation. These are the 'what if' fantasies that we are prone to create when we are feeling at sea. They are born of fear and a sense of loss – loss of meaning, loss of structure, loss of Self.

Speaking of 'feeling at sea', there is a phenomenon that happens in some oceans called 'The Rip'. This occurs when heavy breaking waves create a rapid ebb of water or when a sandbar is breached and the body of water held in front of it rushes to escape. The massive volume of fast moving water in these circumstances is generally confined to the surface layers of the sea and runs directly out from the beach. However, it is incredibly powerful and if you happen to be in its grip, you will be swept up and carried out to sea. People who find themselves caught up in The Rip often try to battle their way back to shore but their attempts are useless. The Rip water is too strong and they just become disorientated and exhausted and end up getting dragged along the ocean floor. However, if they let go and allow the current to take them, they will be given safe (albeit frightening) passage along the surface of the water and disgorged at sea where it's relatively calm. They can then swim back to shore safely. Rips are particularly scary because you can be bobbing about gently in the sea in one moment, and catapulted out to sea the next. Rips are not obvious and sometimes you only notice them when you're in them – just like the transformative process. So, this phase of the transformative process is a bit like riding The Rip. Let go and trust it to bring you safely to where you have to be.

Look for structure

Although the general structure of your meaning mesh may be disintegrating now, you are likely to have one or more other structures within it that can remain stable and act as a crutch whilst you grapple with this process. Of course, I am not advocating avoiding issues by hanging on to something that can act as a distraction, but you may want to return to a touchstone for moments of rest and repair. Look at your professional capabilities, your areas of interest, your passions and your creative outlets. Turn to your family, your close friends, your professional helpers. It is to these places and to these people that you need to return from time to time to replenish your spirit and refresh your thinking. You need to hold on to those things that have occupied you happily in the past so that you can breathe awhile. By doing so, you will create sufficient space in your mind for it to process material 'off-line'. In fact, there are moments in this part of the process where you need to get out of your own way. If you don't have a particular passion or hobby, here is a list of activities that will create a safe structure for you whilst your former life view is disintegrated and shuffled – and, if you can have a laugh whilst you are doing it, you will find it immensely therapeutic.

- Belly dancing or ballroom dancing, jive, tap dancing, salsa, ballet
- Painting, history of art, visiting galleries/museums
- Drama, singing, theatre
- Writing prose or poetry, book reading groups
- Gardening, cooking
- Philosophy, history
- Yoga, meditation, Reiki,
- Cranio-sacral, Bowen, or spiritual healing
- Support groups – Alcoholics, Narcotics, or Overeaters Anonymous
- Training and education
- Writing a journal or writing letters that will never be read

Keeping a journal

I have listed writing a journal amongst the suggestions because it is a wonderful way of externalising your thoughts and reading about what you think. It is not everyone's preference but it does help anchor your feelings and identify what is going on for you. When you read your writing, you will find all sorts of interesting and surprising material that will assist you in your process. It will also be interesting to look back upon the early part of your journey when you have moved through all the stages. It will emphasise how far you have come and allow you to recognise and celebrate your achievements. Having said this, some people never re-read what they've written. The act of writing it down is sufficient to concretise what's happening in their mind.

Mary had lived in an abusive household as a child and had become afraid of silence because it forewarned trouble. When her parents fought, they fought violently, but at least she knew that they were both still alive. When there was silence, however, she was afraid that her mother was either unconscious or dead. At these times, she used to sit on the edge of her bed and hold her breath so that she could hear any noise that would suggest life in her parent's room. After her parents divorced, Mary acquired a step-father who was also abusive, so this pattern was reinforced. As a grown woman, Mary volunteered to be on the end of a telephone for a helpline. She became conscious that when there was silence on the line, she would jump in to get things going again. By breaking the silence, she felt, it would make everything 'normal'. However, she soon recognised that this was a response she'd learned as a child and that it was not helpful to her clients to have her control the conversation when they needed the silence to get their thoughts together. Slowly, she was able to let go of the meaning she'd placed on silence and learn to live with it. I'm giving you this background because it was through journaling that Mary was able to bring this pattern to light and address it. Indeed, she talked more roundly of keeping a journal and the value it brought her. Just being able to read her own words from an objective standpoint and see the patterns and linkages in her thoughts was helpful. As someone who re-read many of her passages, she was also able to trace her progress and get a measured sense of the distance she had travelled on her journey.

In a similar vein, Claire, who was violated by her father as a very young girl, wrote letters. She wrote many letters. Mainly to her father but also to other people she wanted to say something to but felt unable to. Because she had no intention of sending them, she was able to let her feelings flow onto the paper and articulate what she really thought without restriction or the need for censorship. At the end of her writing, when she had finished saying what she had to say, she burned all the letters. This represented her intention to release her attachment to the past and was symbolic of the closure she felt having expressed her feelings. Afterwards, she said she felt cleaned out and able to move on.

Importing structure into your life at this stage of the process is purely to achieve some balance, or at least, establish an anchor where part of who you are can be re-experienced and re-confirmed. Too much external structure can negate the creative work you are being encouraged to do so try not to be too obsessive about the distractions you put around yourself.

What do I believe?

Whilst you are safely anchored in another area of your life or through a familiar and loved activity, it is helpful to get a good understanding of the meaning mesh that has coloured your view of the world and orchestrated your reactions and behaviours. You have already identified the old coping strategies that you adopted in order to protect yourself, but this is more than that, it is about being able to understand your meaning mesh and take an active part in its dissolution and reconstitution. As your meaning mesh dissolves, thoughts and fears will rise to the surface and it is tempting to turn away from these or block them out altogether. However, they are signals to guide you to a fuller understanding of yourself. So, if you feel yourself contracting against a comment, a person or a situation, ask yourself what it is telling you. Ask 'Who?', 'What?', 'Where?', 'When?' and 'Why?' questions and coach yourself into gaining a fuller grasp of your patterns and the reasons for them. What you are doing is using your doubts and fears to take you into your inner territory. For this reason, try and see them as helpful, follow them and see where they take you.

You may have to dig quite deep for the causal factors that were responsible for laying down the patterns in your psyche but don't worry, you are not going to dwell in your own dark recesses for long. I am not advocating wallowing in memories of trauma, just notice the causal event and choose not to allow it to trigger reactions in you automatically. It is very likely that the 'logic' you used to create your meaning mesh in the past no longer holds true and, as a result, it can't be used as a means of viewing the world in the present. Hopefully, the threat that you are protecting yourself from will have disappeared a long time ago and you have merely failed to re-fabricate your meaning mesh to accommodate this change.

Think differently about things

Although I suggest you 'choose' a new way of thinking, I do not say this blithely or uncaringly. It is popularly, and scientifically, believed that our thoughts carve physical grooves in our brain. This natural channel, along which our thoughts flow, is an efficient short-circuit that is designed to prevent us from having to create new thought patterns each time we respond to an experience. However, every time the short-circuit is used, it reinforces our automatic response by deepening the groove. This is done without our conscious intervention and, with this in mind, it is easy to see why we feel unable to control our thoughts. Indeed, by the time we engage our brain, our thoughts have already been thought for us! To be able to see and respond to the world differently, you literally have to carve a new channel that encourages your thoughts to flow in the direction of your choice. Now, instead of your thoughts managing you, you are managing your thoughts.

There are several techniques that might prove helpful in this case. Positive affirmations are one way of re-educating the brain and reinforcing new beliefs. The intention is that eventually, these beliefs will take over the default mode of thinking. It is important, when creating your positive affirmations, to articulate them as if they were already the truth, and to use affirmations that do at least feel possible to you.

"I am happy and confident in my work."

"I am slim, beautiful, healthy and filled with happiness and joy."

"I am loved and held safely in my life."

"I am worthy of receiving gifts and pleasures."

"I am fulfilled and successful in my work."

A work colleague and friend of mine used a particular positive affirmation over and over again to build her confidence. I often heard her say "Looking good! Feeling fine!" as she purposefully walked from one meeting to the next. It made her stand well and walk assertively.

To begin with, you may feel embarrassed and undermine your positive affirmations by murmuring them with no conviction. You may also make quiet, self-accusatory statements like "Who do you think you're kidding?!" Or "Like Hell I am!" However, it is no good hedging your bets by saying your positive affirmations whilst holding on to the belief that the technique won't work. Because you are thinking negative thoughts on the inside, you will find that you sabotage your efforts and create the wrong groove. So, believe, speak and succeed!

Visualisation

Visualisation is another useful tool for changing the way you perceive the world.

A different feature of the brain's function is that it interprets the world through symbols, images and pictures and it connects feelings to these. When recalling situations or events, the brain retrieves information about the past and presents it as memories in the form of images and feelings. Through the brain's ability to do this, we feel as if we relive our memories along with all the consequent feelings that were experienced when they were laid down. Indeed, in this way, we can continuously relive our traumas and taunt ourselves with the original pain. Perhaps we do this to reassure ourselves that we are still alive, sentient beings, but then again, perhaps we could enjoy being alive, sentient beings by evoking and re-experiencing happy memories instead.

Just as our brain can represent the past to us graphically, it can also conjure up the future and play with what is to come. In fact, the concept of past and future is irrelevant as far as the brain is concerned because it can only function in the present; the images of the past and the future are illusions, they do not have substance and form, they merely reflect it, as does a mirror. And, of course, we know that we are not our reflection. A reflection has no substance or form. It is an illusion. If the brain can make an image, therefore, from substance and form, we can create substance and form from an image. So bring to your mind's eye the image of what you want to achieve. Hold onto that image as if it were the truth. See it in colour. Touch it. Feel it. Sense it. Smell it. Revisit it over and over again. Make it your default image. It *will* manifest. Try not to be tempted to undermine your image by running a destructive scenario past it or by recalling damaging statements from your childhood. Hold it as if it were the truth, because it *is* the truth, you have fabricated it; you have created your own reality.

Guided visualisation

Here is a visualisation you can use to help you find some answers to your questions. Make sure you are in a place where you won't be disturbed and where you are comfortable and warm. It is generally best to sit because it keeps you energised but some people prefer to lie down when they take themselves through a guided visualisation.

You can ask someone to talk you through this visualisation. You can record it and play it back to yourself or you can take yourself through it alone and silently. Don't rush it though. Do it thoroughly.

Close your eyes and clear your mind of the noise that is surrounding your day. Put to rest the 'to do' list and think of a question you'd like an answer to. Be very clear about what you'd like to know and be sure that you are open to the answer, which may not be what you expect.

Inwardly ask for protection for your journey and imagine yourself cloaked in white light.

Hold your question in your mind and see yourself at the beginning of a path which heads over a field towards the foothills of a mountain. Feel the light breeze in your hair and the warmth of the sun on your face. Imagine you can feel and hear the brush of the grasses on your legs as you progress along this path. There may be white clouds in the clear blue sky and birds overhead. Look down and see what the path is made of. Is it earthy, stony, rough or smooth? Feel your feet as you place them down and start walking towards the mountain.

As you imagine yourself progressing along the path, you notice a dwelling ahead which is inviting you in. It may be a wooden structure or made of stone. It may be simple or elaborate. Bring to mind what feels natural to you. As you approach the dwelling, you see that the door is open and you get a sense that you are welcome to go in. Sense the atmosphere inside. It is probably cooler now that you are out of the sun.

On a table near the window you see that something has been left for you. It is a gift to take with you on your journey. Go towards it and observe what it is. Inwardly ask the significance of the gift and pick it up. Look at it from all angles and feel the texture of it in your hands. Look around the room and see what else you can see in there. If there is anything else you need for your journey, it is likely to be there willing you to take it. When you have what you need to proceed, turn towards the entrance you used and walk towards and through it. Once outside again, notice the change in light and feel the temperature. See the path stretching out ahead of you. Step onto it and return to the rhythm of the walk that you established before being distracted.

As you walk, you will begin to feel your breath and the exertion required to maintain your pace, particularly as the path starts to ascend, slowly, towards the foothills. Keep walking, feeling the pull of gravity against your body and notice any changes in the path's appearance. Perhaps it is getting a bit rocky now and the grass is giving way to scrub. Keep walking and keep on feeling the exertion as the path takes you across the foothills and onto the lower slopes. Now that the terrain is mountainous, the texture of the path is rockier and you may stumble from time to time. Perhaps the sun is higher now and you are beginning to feel the heat.

Keep walking. See the change in perspective as you climb higher; notice what you can see spread out below you. After a short stop to catch the view, keep on walking up the mountain, higher and higher, noticing all the while any changes that are happening around you. It is a harsher path now than it was when you began your walk. When you reach the summit, all the vegetation will have ceased and only rocks will remain in your immediate vicinity.

Going over the final rise, you see a beautiful temple in front of you. You stop to look at it and observe its size, shape and style. How would you characterise this building? In your mind, practice describing it to someone you are recounting your journey to. Try not to miss any detail that will convey the image and add colour to your story. As you approach the temple, sense its atmosphere, its smell, its sound. Enter through the doorway and use your eyes to explore what is inside. What do you see?

As your eyes adjust to this new environment, you notice that there is someone sitting a short distance from you. You know this person to be a wise one; someone who has your best interests at heart and cares for you deeply. Greet this person and request that you may ask your question. Still holding the object that you picked up from the dwelling at the bottom of the mountain, ask the question that you formed at the beginning of the exercise. Receive the answer and make no comment. This is not a discussion. Thank the being and withdraw from the room and back out through the entrance.

As you exit, remember the answer to the question and commit to carrying it down the mountain as you retrace your steps, all the while observing and feeling the changing landscape and conditions. You might want to rest awhile in the dwelling that you first entered when you began your walk. You may also want to leave your gift so that it is there when your return or it may be used by the next traveller. Finally, leave behind this place and re-join the path to your starting point.

Take some time to 'come to' and allow yourself relative peace and space to integrate your experience. You may want to write it down.

Try not to seek a rescue
Many women are raised with fairy tale dreams of the perfect relationship. The prince, who once was a frog, will find you, kiss you and take you to a happy ever after life. Never is the temptation for rescue as great as it is when you are in turmoil and can't see your way out. The disintegrating stage is such turmoil. Although there are some fortunate people who are able to attract a prince into their lives at such a time it really is not wise to see this as a way of helping you through. When you are in the throes of finding yourself, you will inevitably bring in someone who is attracted to the half-finished version of who you are, not the final product. This could postpone, or worse, arrest your process, leaving your transformation incomplete and unsatisfactory.

Heather was eventually able to view her disintegration positively. Although it didn't come easily to her, she became able to see the value of her defences being broken down as they were preventing her from seeing and feeling things positively. She saw that she had created a sort of prison for her self which kept her stuck in the past and prevented her from moving forward. It also prevented her from accessing her feelings. Because she had silenced these in her childhood to protect herself, they remained hidden and inaccessible in adulthood. Heather said she thought she was having some sort of breakdown but she was not sure what kind of breakdown it was because she was still functioning in her life and able to work things out in her mind. Throughout this part of her process, Heather was able to reappraise the beliefs she held as a child. Such as 'I'm a bad person' or 'I was to blame'. From the light of her current perspective, she was able to see that this couldn't have been the case. She was neither 'bad', nor was she 'to blame'.

If you are open to such a reappraisal, objective observation and reason can challenge these sorts of beliefs, which, if they remain unchecked, can only perpetuate the soul-destroying effects that they have had. As Heather was ready to go to the roots of her beliefs, this kind of breakdown was incredibly releasing for her and a great relief. She didn't have to carry the burden of her beliefs any longer; she could lay them to rest and take the next steps on her journey. As she continued breaking down her defences in this way, she felt freer, more fluid and more optimistic about her destination.

Move the body

As sadness or depression can be a feature of this part of the process, the means of moving things forward is important. Depression is often associated with the 'dark night of the soul'. We talk of 'being in the pit of despair', 'being in a fog', 'feeling our way in the dark', and 'being lost, lonely and alone.' All these expressions conjure up dingy and static images which need to be addressed with the opposite qualities. The saving graces do not claim to resolve deep depression, nor do they intend to trivialise it, but they may help bring a more optimistic dimension to the experience.

To counter the feeling of stuckness, it is important to move the body.

Dancing, running, walking, swimming, keeping fit and yoga have already been suggested but they become even more important when you are working to move through this stage of the process. To create new energy in the body and remind it that it is alive, it needs feeding with oxygen, movement, food and drink – preferably not alcoholic at this stage, as this is likely to conjure up the illusion of a rescue! Any or all of these avenues can be explored and exploited to get you going. In addition, the 'darkness of despair' needs meeting with light and colour. Good illumination in rooms, sunlight if possible and light or brightly coloured clothes are all important for shifting the curse of depression. Also, the feeling of being becalmed in a silent, empty world suggests an antidote which consists of people, relationships and good company. If you don't have a close family or good friends around you, try finding groups that you can connect with and try to fill parts of your day with good conversation and human warmth.

Going for a long walk with a dog (borrow one if you don't have one) can be of great benefit if you don't have easy access to a group of friends or family. Having a warm, breathing body trotting along beside you is really companionable, and it is a being that relies on you to be present, in the moment. If you can walk in nature, along the shore or in a leafy park, so much the better, especially if you can motivate yourself to throw sticks and run with your four-legged friend. But even if your walk is confined to the city, you will be outside in the elements and in the air, both of which will affect and raise your spirit on a subtle level. Of course, in the grip of a depression, physical movement, sound, colour and relationships are the last things that you would naturally seek, but all these are helpful ways of overcoming the insidious and debilitating effects of depression.

You may also want to consult your doctor or complementary heath practitioner to gain assistance during this period of your process, especially if your depression is clinical and needs chemical treatment. Try to avoid your drug of choice, however. It is tempting to lose yourself in alcohol, drugs, or chocolate!

Be mindful

Thich Nhat Hanh is a Vietnamese monk who has written extensively about the Buddhist philosophy; the central tenet of which is mindfulness. In his address to the inmates of the Maryland Correctional Institution in 1999 (reported in his book *Be Free Where You Are*) he says this about anger and despair:

'Without mindfulness in our daily lives, we feed our anger and despair by looking at or listing the things around us that are highly toxic. We consume many toxins each day; what we see on television or read in magazines can nourish our anger and despair. But if we breathe in and out mindfully and realise that these are not the kinds of things we want to consume, then we will stop consuming them. To live mindfully means to stop ingesting these kinds of poisons. Instead, choose to be in touch with what is wonderful, refreshing and healing around you.'

Thich Nhat Hanh advocates beginning the habit of mindfulness by bringing attention to the breath and recommends a breathing meditation to achieve this awareness. Once the breath is mastered, other daily activities like eating and walking can be brought into awareness. From here, it is possible to extend awareness to all aspects of life.

Sark's book *Transformation Soup* (2000) holds many ideas for assisting you in moving through this process. It is bright, cheerful and easy to read. Others in her series are equally readable and enjoyable; these include *Succulent Wild Woman* (1997) and *Eat Mangoes Naked* (2001) (all published by Fireside Books, Simon and Schuster).

STAGE 3 - FINDING YOUR VOICE, BEING HEARD AND VALIDATED

Half way along the road we have to go,
I found myself obscured in a great forest,
bewildered, and I knew I had lost the way.

It is hard to say just what the forest was like,
how wild and rough it was, how overpowering.
Even to remember it makes me afraid.

So bitter it is, death itself is hardly more so;
yet there was good there and to make it clear
I will speak of other things that I perceived.

Study for the Enchanted Forest, Ed Org   **Dante's Inferno (Canto I, 1)**

The study for the Enchanted Forest depicts a sprite blowing a trumpet. She is issuing sweet music, I imagine, to attract the attention of those lost in the forest and to lure them through the chaotic and tangled web that has held them in fear and confusion. The music provides direction, the full moon optimism. Things are getting brighter. Although her eyes are downcast, they are now open.

After entering the disintegrative phase, all the women were keen to give voice to their experiences and most sought professional assistance to help them do this. In every instance, they described the importance of speaking out, being heard, being believed and being validated as they told their stories. Mostly these stories were directed towards a counsellor or therapist who could hold them safely as their emotions began to flow. Occasionally a friend acted as the listening ear but they had to be strong enough to contain the outpouring of feelings and secure enough in themselves not to mount a rescue.

Being believed seemed to be a breakthrough point on the journey to health and one that had to be negotiated before further healing work could proceed. This is not a phase or stage in most other transition models but it was found to be an essential step in this study and may point towards the uniqueness of this particular healing process. It is worth emphasising again that good counselling interventions are not confined to therapy rooms and may be experienced from friends, supportive family members or fellow travellers on the healing journey.

All the women without exception stressed their need to be heard. In today's world, everyone seems to be transmitting messages; no one seems to be listening. Being listened to and received fully is such a great gift. And, of course, you absolutely know when someone is listening to you *really*. Their body language is in line with that of a 'listening person'. This means that you get lots of eye contact, you see them nodding in acknowledgement and you are given space to finish what you are saying with no threat of them jumping in to finish your words or sentences for you. Assumptions and judgements are absent from the exchange and there is no personal agenda on the part of the listener, either of rescue or of projecting and acting out anger of their own. This is how good rapport is built and it carries the tacit message that you are worth building rapport with. Some of the women said that they experienced being heard for the first time in their lives in the therapeutic setting. However, it was not just being heard that was important at this stage, it was also being witnessed and believed.

Rachel, who felt 'unwanted' having been put in care by her mother, talked about needing to be seen as she 'cried out her pain'. And, in the early part of her process, she looked for safe places where she could do this.

Vicky, who was sexually harassed by her father as a young woman, said that she needed someone she could connect with who would trust and believe her. By its nature, abuse occurs behind closed doors and, if accused, the perpetrator can easily deny that it happened. If there were any witnesses, they would necessarily have been collusive, so to be believed is a powerful victory for someone who is trying to put her memories behind her.

Heather, who had been abused by her father and was controlled by her husband, said that just being able to talk about how she felt helped her move on from her experiences.

Emma reflected that she really valued talking to another woman so that she could determine what was normal and what was not. Being able to share her experiences and find that someone understood was very important. When another woman says "Yes, I fully hear and believe you." it is at last possible to shed the doubt and stop questioning yourself. This kind of validation can also be extremely liberating and, perhaps for the first time it becomes possible to believe that there is life beyond the memories. For Emma, too, this went a long way to diminishing her feelings of guilt and isolation.

Claire also felt that it was important to tell somebody about her experiences. She acknowledged that it was hard to find the courage to share her story but felt that giving it to someone else to hold had helped her in her healing process.

This part of the process seems to be pretty much one-way. The women were not seeking sympathy nor were they seeking advice or guidance, they were merely speaking out their experiences; bringing them back into the world where they could be dealt with. It is sometimes hard to find someone who does not react to the sensational nature of the story, pass a judgement or get upset on your behalf. This is not what this part of the process is about. Indeed, it can seriously add to the burden of the story teller. No, this stage is merely about the sounding of memories; bringing them out from the dark and reducing the power of them. We attach so much importance to our stories but we need to see them as just that – stories. They are designed to convey messages and evoke a reaction. That's not to say they aren't true or didn't happen but they are not happening now, they are out of date and out of perspective and to hold on to them too tightly can only smother and stultify healthy growth.

If we identify too strongly with our childhood stories as an adult, we can lose ourselves behind them. Indeed, we can learn to recount them to our different audiences in different ways in order to elicit a strong reaction. We can play with peoples' expectations, emotions and responses through stark or dramatically elaborate storytelling. Stories, if unchecked, can take on a life of their own especially if they have been repeatedly rehearsed, either internally, or to a friend or therapist. On the other hand, as time changes and matures us, we may revisit our stories and give them new meaning. We look at things from different angles and with different eyes as we accumulate experience and learn new things from life. Telling our story over and again helps us to explore its boundaries and determine the places where those boundaries interface with the world. Telling our story helps us to make sense but over telling it starts to undermine the healing process. You need to act as your own guardian against this possibility.

It is important to remember, therefore, that we are telling our story for us, not for our audience. Most women found that they told their story as often as they needed to in order to let it go. And, they let it go when they were able to reassure themselves that they were not their story. They were more than their story.

The importance of finding your voice is underscored by the negative consequences of not being able to find your voice. Many of the women on their quest to speak out, be heard and validated, experienced frustrations when therapists were not knowledgeable enough, courageous enough or experienced enough to listen and bring them to a place of *really feeling understood*. This takes us into the complex territory of the relationship between the client and her therapist; if the unconditional acceptance of the client is not in place, it can block the process and lead to frustration and anger.

As well as recognising the need to be heard and validated from the therapeutic and counselling worlds, we also know that effective learning always involves making an experience explicit. When we look back to review and re-interpret an experience, we need someone to agree with our analysis and to endorse our thinking, especially when it opposes a truth that we have previously held. Then we are free to let go of our old perceptions and take a different view about something.

This stage of the process does come with a 'health warning'. There are instances when 'telling the story' is not coupled with seeking health and happiness but with seeking a 'sharp intake of breath' reaction. With such a response, permission is tacitly given to the abused to remain in victim-consciousness. I have already introduced Caroline Myss's concept of 'woundology' where there is a 'reward' for being a victim. It may be sympathy, concern, assistance or any number of other rewards. Whichever one it is, it is a cotton wool-lined prison that links your identity with that of a victim and keeps you where you are. Reflecting on my own experience, I can remember a time when I presented my life tragedies like items on a laundry list; they became 'me'. This was so much the case that I was disinclined to take responsibility for changing the list, especially as I got such a good 'You poor thing!' reaction from those that would listen. In this way, I was validated for my dysfunctional behaviours and not for who I was inside – until I heard myself tell it once too often and was repelled by the sound of my own voice! On a softer note, this repetitive 'telling' is preparing the ground for more reflective and transformative work.

Finding voice, being heard and being validated is not just confined to telling the story. Indeed, validation may come in the form of a positive reinforcement for something you did well. This has the added advantage of creating a structure that can hold you when all else is failing and building self-esteem at a time when it is probably very low. Being accepted as an effective and valuable person is often a surprise to those who have been conditioned to see themselves in the poorest possible light. But the sun is no less effective when it shines in dark corners than it is when it dances freely across landscapes. It does not reserve its best rays for special occasions nor does it concentrate its efforts for only truly great people. For sure, it has no half measures. So, your dark corners too can benefit from the inevitability of the sun's warm blessings which can be illuminated and healed instantly. Any life filled entity, whether it be vegetable, animal or human, will spring towards its potential as soon as it has the chance.

Kate, who had been sexually abused by her father and brother after her mother died, talked of the importance of being validated by someone that she respected and admired as a means of changing the way she perceived herself. Like many others, Kate had gone into training to expand her professional horizons and build some autonomy in her life. She was much more successful than she ever thought she could be and was surprised when her trainer asked her to step in and teach for her. This challenged her self-belief completely because Kate had such respect for her trainer and thought her to be very talented and special. After this invitation, Kate could no longer hold the belief that she was worthless, useless or hopeless because that would imply that the person she respected so much was equally worthless, useless and hopeless. For Kate this was a small step which led to a dramatic outcome in terms of changing her self-perception.

Saving graces: Finding your voice, being heard and validated

'We are all longing to go home to some place we have never been — a place half-remembered and half-envisioned we can only catch glimpses of from time to time. Community. Somewhere, there are people to whom we can speak with passion without having the words catch in our throats. Somewhere a circle of hands will open to receive us, eyes will light up as we enter and voices will celebrate with us whenever we come into our own power. Community means strength that joins our strength to do the work that needs to be done, arms to hold us when we falter, a circle of healing, a circle of friends and someplace where we can be free.'

Starhawk

When you are at the stage of finding your voice and being heard, it is vital that you find someone to talk to who you trust completely. Someone with whom you can commune; who will receive you, support you and listen to you as you speak what's on your mind. An interested and supportive person will anchor you as you articulate your thoughts, explore different perspectives and try out new ways of seeing things. They will provide you with a touchstone; a place to which you can return to renew your energy and to reorient yourself. Having someone like this to go to, creates a safety net and a structure to replace the one that has been lost in the chaotic stage of disintegrating.

Choose a confidante

This is not the moment to confront the person against whom you hold anger or resentment. An intervention of this nature when you first 'find your voice' carries a high risk of failure and is rarely satisfactory. It is helpful to find someone who will listen to you respectfully and compas-sionately and can be trusted to keep your confidentiality. They should not be someone who likes to sensationalise a story and gossip to others, nor should they be someone who is likely to get angry on your behalf. People often feel that in order to show sympathy or concern they have to make an emotional investment in what you say, but this is not helpful. A witness is what is needed; a loving, holding witness who will validate you and enable you to find a way of moving forward but who will be able to step away once the story has been told. This may be a friend, a therapist or a counsellor. Whichever, it is someone that you choose, not someone who chooses you. If you find that you cannot trust the person that you have chosen to work with, or that the chemistry between you is uncomfortable, choose again.

Many people who have been negated over and over again find this very difficult because their resultant dysfunctional behaviours make them unable to make these sorts of choices, but this stage is too important to risk getting it wrong. So explore your prospective counsellor's operating approach first. Ask them how they work and reassure yourself that you are going to be held safely, in an environment where condemnation and judgement are absent and where your experience will be positive and supporting. Use your intuition to confirm your choice. How does it *feel* to be with them?

Emma reinforces this point by saying:

'The therapist was clear about her boundaries. She was clear about what she was willing to engage in and she stuck to what she said. Even when things went slightly wrong, she was still very open and clear about her own processing so there was nothing hidden in that relationship. When I challenged anything with her she was very willing to reiterate her position on things and that allowed me to start trusting her.'

Family, friends and communities are wonderful for making you feel safe, even if you choose to keep your story hidden. It is worth 'stock-piling' validations of any sort in order to help you feel confident in yourself. You might want to focus on something that you are very good at so that you receive lots of compliments for your work or contribution. This will help carry you into those areas where validation is less accessible and give you a general feeling of self-worth.

Use your voice

Finding voice not only rests on the ability to speak out, but on using the voice effectively in speaking out. Often, when we are uncertain, threatened or nervous, our voice is not projected well and our tone and pitch betrays the messages we are tying to hide. We might speak from the throat and strangle our words, or we might speak in a very quiet diminutive way because we are unsure of what we think or how our message will be received. These are protective behaviours and even though we are speaking out from a technical standpoint, we are unlikely to be *truly* heard. The saving graces that you could employ to challenge these behaviours include singing, chanting or shouting; anything that encourages you to put words, sounds and volume where your mouth is!

It is important, at this stage, for you to take responsibility for your thoughts and messages because unless you can access and convey these clearly, you will find it difficult to move on. Singing is a particularly good activity because not only do you have to enunciate your words and make them clearly audible, you are also trained to use your breath and body as vehicles to convey your message. It may feel a little inhibiting to begin with but you will find that hearing your own voice is powerful and the energetic movement that you will experience from singing will be extremely beneficial. This is true for chanting and shouting too. By engaging in these activities, you will find that your voice will fill those bits of you that have been vacated through fright or harm.

You might like to try wearing a blue gemstone around your neck. Lapis lazuli, blue topaz, aquamarine, turquoise or sapphire, are all attributed with amplifying the power of communication. Have fun choosing yourself a nice decorative gemstone or crystal that will give you confidence as you speak.

The essence of finding voice is that you objectify that which is subjectively held and thereby, make it concrete. In its concrete form, you can start doing something with it. Once you have form, you can move it about, like jigsaw puzzle pieces, until a picture begins to emerge.

By finding voice, you also find language. If you can bring to mind the feeling of telling somebody something for the first time, you may recall that the words and expressions were hard to find. Yet when you told a different somebody that same something for the first time, you may equally well recall a feeling of fluidity. Having already been through the process of finding the right language, your telling was smoother, more expressive and more effective.

STAGE 4 - MEANING-MAKING

To be conscious of Being, you need to reclaim consciousness from the mind.
This is one of the most essential tasks on your spiritual journey.

The Tangled Forest, Ed Org   **Eckhart Tolle**

Making meaning involves disentangling ourselves from the way we have made sense of our lives in the past and finding a new way of looking at things. We literally have to cut a different path through our minds to reveal the new possibilities and opportunities that exist for us. It is like finding our way through a tangled forest; climbing over fallen trees, slipping on mossy twigs and freeing ourselves from the thorns that clutch at our legs. Dante uses the imagery of the forest to signify the challenges he encounters on his journey through hell.

Half way along the road we have to go,
I found myself obscured in a great forest,
Bewildered, and I knew I had lost the way.
It is hard to say just what the forest was like,
How wild and rough it was, how overpowering;
Even to remember it makes me afraid………
The Divine Comedy, Canto I, Dante 1283-1321

Just as Dante uses metaphor to describe the challenges of his journey, Heather also makes connections through metaphor:

'It's like being a jigsaw. You're all the pieces thrown down and you need to look at each piece to see where it fits into the picture.'

This is such a powerful statement because in a few short sentences it indicates the deconstruction, examination and reworking of the meaning mesh. It also speaks for many of the other women as they try to clarify their thoughts, understand the patterns of their behaviours and seek meaning in their experiences. This is a productive phase where women face the past and make sense of it so that they can move forward in their lives in a positive way.

When examining the past, it is important not to get emotionally entangled in the memories, but to view them from a detached standpoint and a safe distance. Let them speak to you but don't let them consume you. This requires objective thinking and a fair amount of discernment and discipline as you sift through and sort out what is relevant to you now and what is not. It is so easy to get sucked into the feelings that your memories evoke and perhaps to feel yourself getting swept up in them as if you were still there in the moment that they were laid down. If you feel yourself slipping back in this way, anchor on something that is present for you. It may be your work, your child, the impetus of your day. Whatever you focus on, make sure it reminds you that you have left the past behind and that it cannot reach you where you are unless you let it.

When you apply discernment to your thinking, it may help you to see it as a three-pronged activity which is made up of a) the ability to receive new information, b) to pick out those bits that are relevant and c) to make deductions or take action based on clear, original and unprejudiced thinking. As busy and mostly distracted people, we often react to trigger-words within pieces of information and find ourselves rushing off down a path that we have been along before.

In the same way that I described in the *Saving graces* section of the *Disintegrating* stage, our clear thinking is short-circuited in favour of fast and efficient mental processing. However, we can miss important contextual information if we only alight on those pieces that we recognise immediately. We need to look at the complete picture afresh each time to ensure that we have picked up all the relevant bits of information and keep our eyes and ears open for anything that we may have missed before or that may be new. Having discernment opens up a whole new vista that leads us into rich territory that allows us to explore more fully. Such an exploration cannot help but lead us into our own mystery and wholeness. But to do this we must let go of our attachment to, and investment in, what we believed to be 'true' because to perpetuate this 'truth' only keeps us in the same place where we are defined as we have always been defined. So, our challenge is to think freshly, incisively and curiously about our past so that we can see things differently, gain new insights and arrive at a new perspective.

The twelve priests, imagination and transformation

The power of challenging previously held thoughts and beliefs was illus-trated in quite a dramatic way by the findings of a researcher in Australia who worked with twelve priests who had decided to renounce their vows in favour of marriage. Through reflection, discernment and deep thought they were able to cast their minds back over their lives and revisit their choices and the reasons for them. Each priest captured his thoughts in autobiographical form, which helped him to see his thinking more objectively. For this community of people, autobiography enabled them to open their minds and hearts in much the same way as journaling. In these moments of openness and non-attachment, they were able to access their unconscious minds, which offered them deeper truths about who they were. Once these deeper truths had emerged, further exploration ensued and they gained greater certainty about the need to change their life direction. As a result, they were able to let go of a very strong affiliation to a belief system in favour of a new and different life script. What this seems to be saying is that we hold the potential to discover more and more about ourselves in our unconscious minds and that this rich vein can only be tapped through our imagination, perhaps as we write our story. You might like to try this for yourself.

Stillness

It is often tempting, when on the trail of an insight, to worry away at it incessantly until you find understanding. However, the process may be more efficient if you find time to enjoy periods of relaxation which are free from focused and determined thought. This is one of the doorways to the unconscious mind and, in the space that is created, it can get on with its business uninterrupted.

This brings us to the idea of 'stillness' which suggests gently side-stepping yourself to allow the hidden part of your mind to work its wisdom. It is hard, sometimes, to get out of your own way but it seems to be an effective way of allowing new ideas and insights to bubble up and make themselves felt. Three of the women found themselves driven into stillness by their process. Heather would sit for hours just looking at a wall. Initially, she might just have sat down for a cup of coffee, but later she would find that two or three hours had passed.

Kate often sat for long periods while her mind went off duty and Vicky, after sitting awhile, would find that she had entered a meditative state, which took her into protracted periods of stillness. It seems that none of these women entered stillness with conscious intent. Instead, they found that their process drove them into it. However, to do this consciously enables you to be in control of the process rather than the other way around. Of course, not everyone will be attracted by the idea of meditation but it is a useful skill to master because as well as creating a space for stillness and clarity of thinking, it also revitalises the body. Spending time just sitting around quietly and letting thoughts enter and exit your mind is a good thing!

When discussing their unexpected entry into stillness, Heather, Kate and Vicky put it down to having over-intellectualised their experiences and having reached the limit of their mind's tolerance. So, their minds just stopped processing thought consciously for a while. Although it was unbidden in these cases, the act of stilling the mind and dropping into a deeper inner space allowed these women to experience the feelings that would otherwise have been talked over and rationalised away. Our feelings might be likened to a lightning conductor that connects us to our vulnerabilities and fears, and because they are painful, we tend to distract ourselves from experiencing and re-experiencing them.

If the journey to personal truth is to be transformational, it seems that feelings cannot be excluded. Their alchemical power must be unlocked and given the freedom to illuminate and transform meaning. To allow this to happen, you need to get your mind out of the way and allow your feelings to rise to the surface and pass through you without comment. You can notice them, and respond to them, perhaps with tears, but you must not get in the way of your own process. By silencing your mind and entering stillness, you can release yourself to your feelings and let them seek out the corners that have atrophied or died. Even though life may have mistreated you, you will find the very best of yourself at the heart of your being and you will be guided there through your feelings, your fears and your pain. What's more, you will learn to recognise your contractions as signposts on the journey. If you respond to a situation like a sea anemone does when you prod it with a stick, you are being given a valuable message. If you react negatively to a person, reject an idea or recoil from an experience, then you are being told something about yourself; it is revealing a deeper truth within you.

This does not mean seeking out pain or remaining with it for long and drawn out periods. It means noticing the pain, understanding the meaning and letting it go. Meaning is negotiable and the meaning we place upon experiences and events is just one of the many interpretations that are available to us. It is just what happens to make sense to us at the time. If we have interpreted something as being painful and we hold that thought, it will always be painful. However, there is always the option of re-interpreting it so that it doesn't cause us pain. This is more easily grasped intellectually than it is to do because many of our responses are ingrained and habitual. When you start being aware of those 'here I go again!' feelings, you will be able to start thinking about how to change your responses. Changing your responses will mean recasting the meaning you have placed upon a situation and determining how you would prefer to see and respond to it. Your engrained reactions, your doubts and fears, are guides on your journey – not occasions to beat yourself up. Let your observations breeze through you as lightly as possible and allow them to place your attention where it needs to be placed.

Although we have seen that meaning-making is largely an intellectual exercise, it is guided by feelings, instincts and intuitions. A balanced combination of all these information highways is essential if a new way of looking at things is to be found. The danger of getting stuck in intellectualisation is that it can lead to 'wheel spin' – that dreadful feeling of going over and over the same thing and not finding a way out. As thinking beings, we are highly efficient at creating intellectual tactics to avoid moving to the next stage of our process, which may be messier, more emotional and tainted with fear. A reluctance to drop from thinking into feelings will hold you mid-way through your process. Those who have passed along the way will have recognised the importance of facing the areas that they have avoided in the past. This is not about subjecting yourself to a re-run of your past experiences, but using your inner knowing to reveal the places that sadness, rejection or pain resides. With consciousness and courage, your incisive mind can cut through and dissolve the fears that have grown around your memories. Using your feelings as a white stick and your thinking as your light, you can tap your way into the cold dark caves where your demons lurk and diminish the shadow they cast over your life. Harold Kushner talks about the importance of going into those dark places. In his book *When Bad Things Happen to Good People*[3], he says that 'Pain is the price we pay for being alive. When we understand that, our question will change from "Why do we have to feel pain?" to "What do we do with our pain so that it becomes meaningful and not just pointless, empty suffering?"

For me, retreating into the mind has been a perennial problem. Blessed with curiosity and a fascination for the mysterious, I have travelled through the nooks and crannies of my mind endlessly. I am known for it. Here she goes again. Another thought, another intrigue. This is what drove me into my research. I so wanted to *understand* what was going on. Now, as I write about this transformative process, I am experiencing it with a vengeance. No longer is it a concept, an intriguing set of data, a pattern that I can share with those who are attempting to interpret their life path, but a real and challenging journey that brings me to my knees and drives me into my sadness and into my senses. I suppose the distraction of my studies was just another elaborate and time-consuming way of putting off the time of my own growth. Although I allowed my intuition and feelings to take me into the theoretical realm of transformation, I didn't take myself there. But I'm there now, facing my shadows and feeling undignified as I do so. However, I have the framework. I do understand. Now is the time to marry the two.

As I write, I am struck by the expression we use when something doesn't make sense to us. We say it is 'sense-less'; a word that conjures up the elements of the mind (logic) and the senses (feelings). We use the same word for both. If our logic fails, nothing makes sense and, if we are not in tune with what we feel, nothing makes sense either. Yet when we experience 'sense-less-ness', those of us who revert to intellectualisation tend to go into our heads and read about it or go on a course. Clearly, this was my strategy at the outset of my research. But I notice it was also the strategy that the women in the study adopted. Nearly all of them took themselves to college to gain some further education or they undertook a training that would give them greater understanding of their own journey. This is valuable as it gives a framework that brings clarity to the process, but the *feeling* senses must also be allowed to enter the mix. Meaning is most powerfully made at the interface between our sensitivities and our mind.

Heather found that during her training programme, she was confronted with feelings that erupted unexpectedly. She heard the theory being espoused from the front of the lecture hall and her experiences so obviously matched what she was hearing that her feelings could no longer be contained. The resonance between her mind and her senses was too great as she sat and listened to the disembodied theory of her own life. In her case, the force of her emotional upheaval was equivalent to the amount of energy she had used to suppress it, so it was very distressing for her. Nevertheless, she saw this as a breakthrough on her path as it took her into a new way of graining greater understanding and making meaning.

The clarification process, defined by the mind and feeling combination, is essential for uncovering the reasons for our behaviours. And, once these reasons have been surfaced, we can work upon them, take more control of them and participate in our lives in a more robust and authentic way. Indeed, dramatic personal changes are possible when we become aware of the assumptions we make and the reactions that are triggered by events. When we can challenge these assumptions and arrest our automatic responses, we can deepen our relationships and learn to act authentically in the world.

We have looked at stillness as a means of tapping the unconscious.

Clearly, there is a role here for meaning making through dreams. Dreams are graphic representations of what's going on out of consciousness and they often occur vividly during the early stages of the transformative process. Although much has been written about the symbolism of dreams, the truth is, their significance is only known to you. Whatever you think they mean is what they mean. You are closest to the symbolic resonances within your own mind so use your intuition to understand what your dreams are telling you.

Vicky described a dream she remembered having during the early stages of her healing. For her, the symbol of the spider was significant because it represented feeling trapped and powerless. If one was in her path, she could neither step on it nor over it because both would be too frightening. This is how she relayed her dream. "I had a nightmare about clearing a room. I was taking old plaster off the walls and making sure all the corners were scraped out ready for the new plaster. There was a vast spider in one of them. It was terrifying but it was preventing me from completing my task so, not having any other tactic to deal with it, I had to Hoover it up. I extended the pipe as far away from my body as possible and directed the suction over the spider. Thankfully, it didn't run away and I got it. I could hear the Hoover race as the spider was drawn along the length of the hose. It made a horrible fluttering and cracking sound. At one point, it sounded as if the spider had blocked the way and the sound of the Hoover squealed as a vacuum built up behind it. Then it returned to normal when the Hoover swallowed the spider with a sudden gulp. I let the Hoover run so that it couldn't come back down the hose again. I woke palpitating and feeling really vulnerable. I think it was because I was facing so many of my fears in therapy and trying to make sense of them all."

Saving graces: Meaning-making

If architects want to strengthen a decrepit arch, they increase the load that is laid upon it, for thereby the parts are joined more firmly together. So, if therapists wish to foster their patients' mental health, they should not be afraid to increase that load through a reorientation toward the meaning of one's life.

Victor Frankl

The clarification process is one that can be assisted in many ways. Saving graces come thick and fast as you begin to focus your attention on the patterns of your own behaviour and notice the things that you do and the choices that you make. Weaving these together will allow you to see what makes you the way you are. There will be a common thread, an underlying belief or set of beliefs that create the meaning you take into your life and it will be manifest through the choices you make and the things that you do.

Naming and sharing

Meaning-making is firstly about naming. Merely naming something; a thing, a place, a behaviour, a pattern, enables you to make meaning. Hearing yourself talk about something, sharing the meaning you've placed upon it, refining this meaning and coming to an agreement about it enables you to develop a language that symbolises what you think and believe. Then it is about arriving at an agreement about the name. The language we use and the significance we place upon words define the type of conversations we have. We can have our conversations on a superficial level where the words convey observations or messages that are momentary or instructive, or we can delve deep and explore the different layers of meaning that exist in our language. Because personal transformation gouges a deep groove, the naming and sharing is powerful and therefore must be done in a safe and trusting environment where the exploration is respected and contained. Then it can be exciting, revealing and releasing. Having a passionate and meaningful exchange enables you to slip through the sliding doors between confusion and understanding and enables you to enter a new world of being.

Language is not the only way through, however. To find meaning, it is not only helpful to 'hear' it through discussion but also to 'see' it through journaling and 'feel' it through experience. You might say that seeing, hearing and feeling gives you a 360 degree experience of meaning. So try to engage in activities that bring in a new sensory dimension. Music, art and drama all qualify as these creative media contain lifetimes of practise and wisdom.

Naming and sharing is how we weave the tapestry of our meaning mesh and it seems that this is a particularly important activity for women. This is because they are challenging the meaning that they created in the past – or had created for them – and it can feel quite disconcerting as old meaning is lost and new meaning is found. Fixed meaning is an illusion. It is up for negotiation and re-negotiation all the time. Nothing is fixed. When something can't be named or shared it is almost impossible to find the meaning of it.

Find meaning through art

The concept of a meaning mesh may seem rather abstract to you and you may find yours hard to get hold of. Indeed, it would probably be tough to describe it to someone if they asked you what yours looked like. If you are having this sort of difficulty, one helpful way of bringing it to light is to draw or create a collage of your life. Your meaning mesh is what holds it all together and it will be implied by your artwork.

Create a collage of meaning

Using a large piece of paper, lots of free expression and intuition, create a map that tells the story of where you have come from and where you are presently.

You could use the metaphor of a road, river or railway line to convey the sense of your journey. Put in the milestones, crossroads and sign-posts that you followed (or ignored) along with the gifts or chances you were given. Indicate the barriers or obstacles that you had to overcome and any significant points along the way. Decorate your map as you see fit. Try not to censor the images you use to depict your experiences. Go to town. Use colour, pictures cut from magazines or newspapers, glitter, paint and any other medium that takes your fancy. Be as inventive as you can. Recall the joy of painting as a child when there were no restrictions or expectations placed upon you.

Once you are satisfied with your artwork, stand back (admire it!) and speculate upon its meaning. You may be able to identify the golden (or tarnished) thread that holds your experiences together relatively easily; or the ravines that hold them apart.

It is often useful to find someone to whom you can voice the meaning of your creation. Get them to ask you what the images mean, why you have used a specific colour, what was going on in a certain place. Then get them to probe the beliefs that led you into a particular activity or in a certain direction. They could ask you "Tell me more…" type questions that encourage you to reflect, but don't let them participate too much in the discussion. It is *your* reflection, not theirs. However, as you respond to their questions, you will hear yourself respond from your belief system; it will be as if your unconscious is speaking to you – and you will see your life laid out before you, pictorially, giving you an overview so far and the meaning that holds it together.

This work is founded on the belief that the unconscious mind plays a powerful part in determining our thoughts, feelings and actions. Although we may not be aware of them, the injunctions from our unconscious send us on a life journey and invite us to take certain courses of action. However, these injunctions are often conditioned for us in our childhood years or silenced by interference from others. So, our conscious 'foolish' mind, or ego, dominates the unconscious and eclipses the efforts of this wise mediator to inform who we are and how to express ourselves. The result is that we are left feeling fractured and disjointed on an inner level. By revealing the images that inhabit the unconscious mind, we can understand them, integrate them and allow them to make new meaning for us. In doing so, we also gain deeper knowledge of our truth, our essential Self.

Often, when tapping our unconscious through art and imagery, we find that our inner world does not reflect our outer world at all. The picture we hold of ourselves in our mind, the one we invest in and build upon, does not reflect 'our truth' – the picture that is held in the deeper part of our mind. This dissonance is often felt as a lack of purpose, of being in the wrong place, of doing the wrong things, of not being true to ourselves, of being on the wrong footing, or any other such feeling. By using images to reveal what's in our subconscious, we can begin to see where the gaps are and what our losses look like, for they will feel like losses. Somewhere, we will be mourning for the person we once were; the person we have hidden under our protective behaviours. Accessing your unconscious can be quite an emotional experience but it is a powerful way to make clear that which is hidden from you so it is well worthwhile going through the exercise. However, do make sure some trusted support is on hand.

Sit on your own shoulder

Another suggestion for deepening self-understanding is to observe yourself consciously as you react to, and interact with others. Imagine yourself sitting on your own shoulder, watching quietly as you engage with people. Watch yourself kindly but honestly. Try not to fudge what you see, whether it be good or bad in your opinion. Make your observations objective and impartial. You are only collecting information. Notice when you get those 'familiar feelings'. They could include feelings of being criticised, judged or attacked, or they may be felt as rising panic or excitement when a situation is accented or heightened in some way. They could manifest as a total evacuation of confidence. See if you can capture the essence of what is going on for you and why this has occurred. Ask yourself what or who is conditioning your response. Does it remind you of anything? Placing your attention on yourself like this may feel a little uncomfortable at first but you will soon get used to watching yourself in your daily routine. Soon you will find that it feels quite natural and you will be wiser for it.

Do something different

At this stage, it is very easy to become an obsessive thinker, twirling things round and round in your mind to no avail. To counter this, try to take your mind offline for a while. Take time out to do something you've never done before. Jettison all your immediate concerns and mindful wrestlings and take yourself to the seaside, to see movie, a show or a play. Learn something new, not necessarily related to self-discovery. Perhaps a pottery class, watercolour, photography. Anything to help you step off your path for a while. Sometimes, when we steel the wisdom of the process and try to force things to happen at speed, we actually end up stopping ourselves from proceeding. It is ironic that the more you attend to something, the more elusive it becomes. However, carry your intention to learn about yourself around with you gently and be vigilant when the messages come back to you.

Meditate

Meditation is a good way of creating a structured activity when everything else is falling apart. It is also extremely good for clearing the mind and allowing natural wisdom and insights to emerge from the subconscious. It has been found that meditation can increase the body's natural defences against disease and depression and it also increases physical energy and brain activity. Many people have adopted this approach successfully in their lives and are reaping the benefits. Meditation doesn't have to involve sitting cross-legged for hours as you clear your mind of all thought. Meditation can be done in many ways, through physical activity or though stillness. Techniques range from power yoga, which results in you breaking into a sweat, to transcendental meditation, which is still and silent. Chanting is good for finding voice and it can also be useful for clearing the mind and channelling energy away from constant brain activity. It is important to find a technique that works for you and that you can fold into your daily routine relatively easily. Even two minutes a day of your chosen method has proven to be effective.

A breathing meditation

Sit with a straight back, either cross-legged or on a chair with your feet shoulder-width apart. (The straight back is important because it allows energy to flow freely up and down your spine and around your body. You will also be able to fill and empty your lungs without restriction.)

Breathe consciously. (This distracts you from filling your mind with other thoughts.) Focus on the feeling of the air entering your nostrils and filling your lungs. Notice if the air entering is cooler than your body temperature. Feel the effects of this cool air around the entrance to your nose.

Take the breath deep into your body and allow your belly to swell with the volume of inhaled air. Hold your breath for a little while and then breathe it out, deflating your belly. The filling and emptying of your belly should create a smooth movement, like a waveform. Be aware of the warmth the air picks up as it passes through your body.

Try counting your breaths in this conscious state and see how far you get. If you want a measure, just getting to five to begin with is a real triumph. If you flounder, start again and see again how far you can get the second time. Your aim is to try and increase this number every day and succeed in getting your mind out of the way! If thoughts intrude, notice what they are and then release them without judgement and return to your breathing.

Some people find it helpful to envision smoke being exhaled with the out breath. It is a more tangible focus. Others like to meditate to tapes or music. This is fine as long as it doesn't encourage distracting thoughts from entering the mind. Done effectively, this technique can be very relaxing. When you have finished, sit quietly for a short while and allow the exercise to be taken into your body and integrated.

There are lots of self-help tapes and books on meditation. You might like to explore them and see if any appeal to you. Or perhaps, you could join a yoga or meditation class. It is sometimes easier to get started on these more disciplined activities in community with others where support is available and experiences and tips can be shared and exchanged.

STAGE 5 - CONTROLLING: MAKING CHOICES AND MANAGING BOUNDARIES

And there she lulled me asleep,
And there I dream'd—Ah! woe betide!
The latest dream I ever dream'd
On the cold hill's side.

I saw pale kings and princes too,
Pale warriors, death-pale were they all;
They cried—"La Belle Dame sans Merci
Hath thee in thrall!"

I saw their starved lips in the gloam,
With horrid warning gaped wide,
And I awoke and found me here,
On the cold hill's side.

Lady with Sword, Ed Org   **John Keats (1795–1821)**

To me, this picture of the Lady with Sword conveys the image of someone who is in control of her boundaries; who can cut through deception and illusion with the sword of her own truth. In the series of pictures that I have chosen to accompany each stage of the process, the women are becoming bolder, their eyes are opening wider and more confidence is present in each image. It feels as if they are increasingly coming into their truth and beauty.

During the controlling phase of the journey, the women talked of finally being able to make choices in their own right and not give their power over to someone else. In the language of (male) developmental psychologists, personal growth leads to increasing levels of autonomy and the desire to define oneself. But the price of defining oneself is high and often, at significant life stages, people ricochet back and forth a bit before finally choosing the 'higher' trajectory of their growth.

The price is high because to define oneself is very exposing. It means showing yourself in a truer light than ever before and leaving behind your protective masks and behaviour patterns. It also can mean leaving behind familiar relationships that have apparently held you safely in the past; *apparently* because they may have been based on a delusion, collusion or illusion!

In many of the instances described by the women in the study, their relationships were the casualties of their growth. This is not uncommon. Just because one member of a partnership seeks new expressive horizons, it doesn't mean to say that the other will follow. In fact, the other might be quite satisfied with the way things were; familiar, acceptable and predictable. They may not want the changes introduced by new growth because it will threaten the status quo and demand an upheaval that they feel is neither desirable nor necessary. When there is an unequal pull like this, it is quite likely that the relationship will take the strain and the person wishing to retain the status quo will find another who is happy to play their part. This is not to say that relationships necessarily have to be the casualties of growth nor is it a judgement on those that know when they are happy with a situation and wish to continue it, it is just to acknowledge that a person who is experiencing transformative growth may need someone who has the capacity to accommodate their changes and celebrate the flowering of their potential. Some are blessed with partners who are happy to see their loved ones grow and who will adventure with them into new forms of expression and truth. Others, sadly, are not.

It always surprises me when I see weeds growing up through concrete or Buddleia growing on the rooftops of derelict buildings. It seems that nothing can hold these plants back from expressing their full potential. Human beings have this same impetus to grow and express themselves, yet often, this is constrained by the fears and vulnerabilities of others close to us. Sadly, many of us let those who are in our closest sphere hold us back and we learn to 'make do' with the freedoms they allow us. Some of us, if we are fortunate, are able to channel our potential where it is acceptable and derive some satisfaction from doing this. But others of us may feel that we have to smother our potential so that it doesn't threaten or destroy our closest relationships. However, although we can press our potential 'pause' button for a while, if our growth is determined, it will not be paused for long. Eventually, it will push through and if anything gets in its way, it will be removed by the fulsomeness of its own expression. This is when we really embrace the responsibility of being a choosing adult; someone who creates and maintains her own boundaries and makes decisions about how she is going to live her life.

When you start expressing yourself truthfully, you will most likely *feel* it, not *think* it. From this feeling state, you will choose what is right over what is wrong, and *right* will be determined by you, not by somebody else. Your intuition will start guiding you and providing you with self-protection, self-assertion and self-definition. You may appear not to need validation from an external source at all. Instead, you will be able to carve your truth with a new sense of power and enjoy openness to new experiences and novelty.

Health warning!!!!

Although self-possession is one of the attributes of this stage of the process, so too is recklessness; arguably its complete opposite. Recklessness often emerges in response to a new-found and exciting feeling that you 'know' what needs to be done. So, with enthusiasm and bravado, you break through as many barriers as possible with the spirit of cutting a swathe with a machete. As the tangled undergrowth of your former confusion and chaos is felled and flattened, you carve a purposeful path which leads you speedily through the challenges and tasks you have set yourself.

Many of the women that I spoke to looked back over this period with self-deprecating humour and felt that they had rushed into areas where angels would fear to tread. Each woman recounted frightening challenges that they had deliberately put on their path. Holidays alone in sexually predatory countries, solitary adventures in the outback, trekking alone in the Himalayas, adrenalin-charged extreme sports, one night stands with strangers from exotic climes, deep tissue massage with a team sports' physiotherapist... you name it! They were not really being 'irresponsible'; they were merely testing their boundaries and finding their edges.

Some of the women chose to confront their abusers at this point and, with a brazen clarity and fury, they landed heavily, seeking confirmation, apology or recompense. I must say, in no case was this successful so if you do take this approach, be prepared to be disappointed and create some loving, human safety nets for you to fall into.

Having lived within the confines of imposed boundaries, you will, in certain regards, have been prevented from making significant choices and will therefore not be practised at this art. However, you must start making clear choices if you are going to take command of your life. To begin with, you might go to the extreme and put yourself in the way of one of the options listed above, but this probably won't be a sign that you are becoming wantonly reckless – just that you are alive! It is likely, though, to take you into territory that you had never previously thought possible and it may even frighten you. But this time, it is *you* that is choosing to be frightened; it is *you* that is deciding what you want to do and it is *you* that is putting yourself on the line. You may have been 'protected' or you may have protected yourself so ferociously in the past that you didn't know you had the capacity for such extremes. Some of the women reflected back in horror at what they'd done, but mostly, they did so with a sense of satisfaction that they had at least tried it. In fact, many of them continued to test their edges to get a continued sense of their growth and to reassure themselves that they weren't retreating back into their old shells.

If you are to control your boundaries, you will need to know where your boundaries begin and end and taking yourself to the edge is probably the only way you'll be able to see the shape and size of your personal imprint. How do you know what you are like if you don't put yourself into situations that will call on your inner reserves and reveal your resourcefulness and capability? If you always live within the confines of certainty (not that there is such a thing!) and if you always stand back from the edge, you will never really get to know who you are. All you'll get to know is what your fears are and how these shape you. But living in fear is less than a half-life; it is not who you are but who you are not. In the past, you may have behaved small because you knew the dangers of touching or crossing the lines that others had drawn for you. But now, as a bold, breathing and buoyant adult, you have to determine these lines for yourself and manage the inclusion or exclusion of others within your own sphere of being. You may appear gauche at first as you practice this skill. You may let people in too close and find yourself fighting for your space again. You may keep people at bay and find yourself building bridges to reach them again. But over time, you will find that you can hold your lines with clarity and strength. No longer will there be trespassers on your territory. No longer will you be unable to keep people out. You are now your own preserve, and you will preserve yourself.

May I just say that I am not *necessarily* advocating deliberate and foolhardy recklessness. Sometimes, just having a massage or going for a walk by yourself feels reckless to you. If it is not too much of a contradiction in terms, try being reckless gently! Don't over face yourself and put yourself in danger of feeling a failure. Look for early successes so that bit by bit, you can increase your personal footprint on the earth.

Children, particularly teenagers, push the boundaries all the time as they grow. 'How far can I go?' 'How much can I get away with!' 'When will I have to give in?' With these internal questions, they nudge their way out of their comfort zones until they know who they are. What is me? What is not?

So go on, put your edges out there. Do something you've secretly craved to do. Test yourself!

Saving graces: Controlling

God grant me the serenity
to accept the things I cannot change;
courage to change the things I can;
and wisdom to know the difference.
The serenity prayer, Reinhold Niebuhr

Although, with the zeal of new-found strength, testing our own boundaries can appear reckless, it seems to be important to take oneself to the
edge in order to find reassurance that there is no situation that cannot be
managed. Perhaps you would argue that this is the antithesis of control
but strangely, it seems to be the essence of it. It is exactly where control
is in danger of being lost that the reassurance of control can be gained. If
you bring to mind sports such as skiing, base-jumping or sky-diving, it is,
paradoxically, the release of control that enables success to be attained,
albeit with the right equipment. Over-concerned and over-controlled
skiers often hurt themselves because they try to put brakes on the speed
that actually keeps them safe. A skier that releases herself to the elements,
and who is in tune with the varying components of speed and direction,
will have an exhilarating and safe run. In the same way, having amassed
the 'right equipment' – intellectually, emotionally and spiritually – the
women in this study deliberately took themselves into potentially threatening situations in order to test their ability to release control and then
find it.

Again, we consider the possibility that 'real' control is won at the
point at which it is lost. Initially, this can appear to be foolhardy, and
perhaps it is. However, 'practise makes perfect' and as the women moved
through their healing process, they acquired a beautiful self-assurance
that did not require constant proof that they were in control, rather, this
self-assurance existed as quiet, integral knowledge; no showy demonstra-
tions, no brash antics, it just folded itself around them with a female glori-

ousness that spoke of capability, wisdom and confidence.

Although their initial recklessness may have been appeared aggressive, the women did not exhibit high levels of aggression. Indeed, their style seemed to have moved from aggressive – where they were overcompensating for the fear of losing control, to assertive – where they were able to trust in their own resourcefulness.

Be Assertive

An assertive style of communication enables you to honour yourself as well as the person with whom you are communicating. It is not about domination or submission, instead it creates a place of reciprocity where both of you can find voice and be heard without either one losing their definition. This is particularly important for those of us who were trained to be 'pleasers'. We are more likely to see communication as a lose/win battle, with us being the losers. This is because we were made to believe that our place in the world was dependent upon us meeting others' wishes. Learning to be assertive, therefore, is recommended as a saving grace at this stage.

Assertive communication develops a number of useful skills that you can take into a much wider context; professional as well as personal. Assertiveness can also help in meeting parenting challenges, especially in the teenage years, as it demands the receipt and consideration of infor-mation, not merely its transmission. A common complaint of teenagers is that: "You're always telling me what to do!" "You just don't understand me!" and "You automatically say no without thinking about what I want!" And, of course, they are often right. An assertive communication style brings many helpful techniques such as active listening, building rapport, negotiating and persuading, presenting ideas, delivering messages and controlling body language. When a teenager feels seen, heard and validated, they too will be able to find themselves. All this and increased confidence too!

To get you started, here are is a framework and a few tips:

Taking an assertive stance is equivalent to stating that you consider yourself of equal value to everyone else; you have the same rights and choices. This does not preclude you from having compassion for others nor does it prevent you from making choices in their favour from time to time, it merely allows you to make those choices consciously.

If you allow others to bamboozle you, you are, albeit unconsciously, conveying the impression of the 'victim' or indicating 'I am not worthy.' This is called the 'passive' stance and it gives others free reign to interpret your acquiescence in whatever way that suits them. It also enables them to use you, to bully you and to get you to do things that you might not wish to do if you were given the space and time to consider its repercussions. As an adult who is considered to be exercising choice, as indeed those that bamboozle you consider themselves to be, you are unwittingly giving them permission' to walk all over you. This is a notorious trait that has been socialised into the female community over millennia!

Sometimes, when we want to stand up to a bully but don't feel that we have the 'right', we turn to what is called a passive/aggressive style of communication. This is the voice or action of the quiet saboteur, the person that hides behind apparently benign or acquiescent messages. Whilst seeming to co-operate, agree with or support someone, these people are actually conspiring to do the opposite. Passive/aggressive behaviour is often seen in incongruent body language or inconsistencies between what is said and what is done. The signs that this style of communication is being used are found in 'leakage'. Whilst saying one thing, the passive/aggressive person is usually sending signals that convey another. Fidgety feet, fiddling with a pen, the loss of eye contact or the over use of gestures may be such signs. A common form of leakage is seen in the person who gives verbal agreement to something whilst shaking their head to indicate disagreement. Because the person exhibiting passive/aggressive behaviour is not taking responsibility for their thoughts or actions it is perceived to be weak. Vengeful and spiteful behaviour falls into this category.

If you take an 'aggressive' stance, what you are conveying is that you consider yourself superior and that your choices and decisions should prevail in all circumstances. This is the stance of the bully; the person who thinks they know best and can determine everyone else's choices and lives for them. Most of us have experienced such a person and many of us have tried at times to adopt the behaviours of this type of person. It does not win friends in the longer term; it only succeeds in meeting your immediate needs, not your enduring ones.

Assertiveness is clearly presented as the most effective form of communication but there are times when the other styles are useful too. If you are being attacked, for example, it may be appropriate to portray the victim in order to minimise any danger or potential damage that may be caused. In a crisis, you may need to adopt an aggressive style and shout a command. However, these other styles of communication should be seen as resources rather than characteristics of your style.

The passive and passive/aggressive forms of communication are typical of those of us who have been bullied or abused. We have 'learned' that we have no power so we drop into passivity to remain safe. By doing this, however, we become a 'sitting duck' for any would be aggressor who passes by.

There are many assertiveness training programmes, books and tapes to help you develop this style of communication. It may be a helpful way of creating a structure that will build your self-esteem and allow you to make the choices that you wish.

Visualisation and NLP

I have already talked about Visualisation as a powerful way of changing the way you think about yourself. But it is also a useful technique to ensure that your behaviours match your aspirations as a confident, self-authoring person. Try to recall those moments when you felt confident and fully empowered. See in your mind's eye what it was you were doing at the time and bring forward the positive feelings of that moment. In

Neurolinguistic Progran...
that together, your min...
have of the world - i...
feelings by pinching together you...
you want to call on these feelings again, you simply ...... the pinching
movement and they will come flooding back to you. There are ma...
books and self-help tapes that can be used to perfect this art. You might
start with *NLP for Dummies* by Romilla Ready and Kate Burton.

Find a role model

When we are bringing ourselves to our truth, we may find it difficult to
know what our truth is. Who am I, *really*? If you are asking yourself this
question, ask who in your network of friends and acquaintances exhibit
the qualities that you admire the most. You may like to consider figures
from history, politics or the celebrity world. You probably won't be able
to identify someone who possesses all the traits you admire, indeed, they
may have some that you find positively distasteful, but at least you will
be able to start sifting the 'good' from the 'bad' in your terms.

Your aim, with this exercise, is to create a composite role model that
gives you a clue about what is true for you. If someone has a particular
style, attitude or belief that appeals to you, then the chances are it reflects
something within you already; something that you may not have
considered to be true about yourself until now. Try making a list of all the
virtues you admire in your pool of inspiring people. If they all came
together, what would they look like? You? Once you have done this, you
will be able to see where to focus your attention, what things to try out
and where they would work best.

Find inspiration to fuel your determination to change

As a pretty, petite child, Linda was considered aberrant by her family, all
of whom were large, extrovert males. (Although her mother was present
throughout her childhood, she was very male in her demeanour and

similarly sizeable.) Instead of being treated as precious, Linda was derided and dismissed. In her isolation, she learned to love reading and to cherish the escape it brought her. As she matured, Linda turned to more classical English literature and eventually studied it at University. Like many, Linda found that her feelings were often expressed through poetry. A poem that was significant for her is **The Second Coming** by W. B. Yeats which I have reproduced below.

The Second Coming

Turning and turning in the widening gyre
The falcon cannot hear the falconer;
Things fall apart; the centre cannot hold;
Mere anarchy is loosed upon the world,
The blood-dimmed tide is loosed, and everywhere
The ceremony of innocence is drowned;
The best lack all convictions, while the worst
Are full of passionate intensity.

Surely some revelation is at hand;
Surely the Second Coming is at hand.

The Second Coming! Hardly are those words out
When a vast image out of Spiritus Mundi
Troubles my sight: somewhere in sands of the desert
A shape with lion body and the head of a man,
A gaze blank and pitiless as the sun,
Is moving its slow thighs, while all about it
Reel shadows of the indignant desert birds.

The darkness drops again; but now I know
That twenty centuries of stony sleep

Were vexed to nightmare by a rocking cradle,

And what rough beast, its hour come round at last,

Slouches towards Bethlehem to be born?

The term 'widening gyre' at the end of the first line conveys the shape of a cone. If you imagine the falconer at the sharp end of the cone and the falcon circling in ever increasing and rising circles above her, there is a point at which control of the falcon (such as it was) is lost. This is conveyed in the third line; 'Things fall apart; the centre cannot hold'. This represents, for Linda, the fall into chaos and the futility of trying to hold on and remain in control whilst things fall apart, yet, as we know, it is in the letting go that strength and freedom can be found.

Another interpretation of the poem sees the falcon as the 'head' or 'intellect' containing logic and thought and the falconer as the 'body' or 'heart' containing sensations and feelings. Metaphorically speaking, perhaps the head and the heart have to express themselves separately in order to know themselves before they can connect and integrate in the image of the Sphinx, which brings these two components together. So for this stage of controlling, and the next stage of integrating, this poem seems to say it all.

Pema Chödrön could also have been inspired by this poem when she titled her book *When Things Fall Apart* which takes a Buddhist view on the pursuit of happiness from a place of chaos and despair. You may find it helpful.

STAGE 6 - INTEGRATING

'The inside has joined the outside so I'm now whole rather than lots of different pieces.'

Alverick the Witch, Ed Org   **Heather**

The image of Alverick the Witch is an interesting one. I liked the conveyance of power and mystery and the fact that Alverick's sword is now a staff, decorated with jewels. She is looking up; her eyes fully open as she waits expectantly for the arrival of the male horseman or knight. She is confident in herself. The enchanted forest, from which she has emerged, is no longer tangled, only a few strong and fully grown trees remain. This stage of integration brings together both sides of the brain, right (creativity) and left (thinking), both aspects of a person's psyche. It also brings together animus (male) and anima (female) as well as strength and vulnerability. Finally, we are getting there!

When we have little understanding of our bad childhood experiences, we may judge that we can't have been loveable because, if we had been, people wouldn't have been horrible to us. So the logic goes. This is an example of linear thinking where a cause is linked to an effect. We were not loveable (cause), so people were horrible to us (effect). At the integrating phase of the healing journey, this kind of thinking is transcended and the cause and effect relationship is put into a wider context. Indeed, we begin to understand that cause and effect thinking is too simple, it doesn't really explain the full complexity of what was going on. Once we recognise this, the cause and effect relationship relaxes and we can give room to a different interpretation. We may have had horrible experiences, but this doesn't mean we weren't lovable. There was something else going on. As we build our knowledge and gain further understanding, we are able to accommodate the possibility that we had horrible experiences <u>and</u> we were, and are, loveable.

As a child, you have the misfortune to experience only half of the story; you know your side of it well enough but you can only speculate on the other. This speculation, based on logical deduction, leads to the natural conclusion that links your horrible experience to your personality – you are not loveable – and it is very likely to colour your adult years until a wider perspective is gained. If you take responsibility for the cause of your experience, this 'fact' is rehearsed over and over again until it is ingrained in your thinking. In this way, you convince yourself that you are at fault and that you deserve people to be horrible to you. Even though you may have this perception you really don't have the full picture; you only have part of it.

The poem *The Blind Men and the Elephant* by John Godfrey Saxe (1816-1887) illustrates this point beautifully:

It was six men of Indostan
to learning much inclined
who went to see the Elephant
(Though all of them were blind),
that each by observation

might satisfy his mind

The *First* approached the Elephant
and happening to fall
against his broad and sturdy side
at once began to bawl
"God bless me! but the Elephant
Is very like a WALL!"

The *Second*, feeling of the tusk
cried, "Ho, what have we here,
so very round and smooth and sharp?
to me 'tis mighty clear
this wonder of an Elephant
is very like a SPEAR!"

The *Third* approached the animal
and happening to take
the squirming trunk within his hands,
thus boldly up and spake:
"I see," quoth he, "the Elephant
is very like a SNAKE!"

The *Fourth* reached out an eager hand
and felt about the knee
"What most this wondrous beast is like
is mighty plain," quoth he:
"'Tis clear enough the Elephant
is very like a TREE!"

The *Fifth*, who chanced to touch the ear
said: "E'en the blindest man

can tell what this resembles most;
deny the fact who can,
this marvel of an Elephant
is very like a FAN!"

The *Sixth* no sooner had begun
about the beast to grope,
than seizing on the swinging tail
that fell within his scope,
"I see," quoth he, "the Elephant
is very like a ROPE!"

And so these men of Indostan
disputed loud and long
each in his own opinion
exceeding stiff and strong,
though each was partly in the right,
and all were in the wrong!

This poem creatively illustrates the point that we often only see a very small part of the whole. By focusing our attention on what is most obvious, what is immediately in front of our eyes, we fail to see the bigger picture; we can't see the elephant!

Integrating is about moving beyond cause and effect relationships, bringing it all together and putting it into a wider context.

The various definitions that can be found on integrating all point towards the act of assimilating large amounts of information so that it makes sense as a whole. It is about getting a clear view of the big picture rather than seeing only little bits, as you do on a jigsaw puzzle piece. From a psychological perspective, these definitions of 'integrating' bring an understanding of how the various cultural, social and experiential influences come together to form our whole personality. Once we can understand this, we can seek harmony between what we experience on the outside and what we know to be true on the inside.

As we are beginning to expect, the integrative stage is not one that can be taken for granted, nor is it permanent. No sooner does it all come together than it seems to fall apart again. The integrating stage then is one that is reached, experienced and lost before being reached again. So, again, although the impression of stages that I have given so far implies linear progress, this is not actually the case. In fact, in the sense that one stage is finished before another begins, it is clear that our passage through the stages is not 'clean' at all. Not only this, but a former stage is sometimes experienced in one dimension of our life whilst a later stage is experienced in another. It is quite common for you to be going through a transformation in the personal arena after having already been through a professional transformation. Or one might trigger the other!

We can liken this transformative journey to a physical journey. As we tread our linear path and look around ourselves, the landscape changes over time and sometimes looks very different at the end of the journey from how it was at the beginning. However, as we progress, the features of the landscape don't appear and disappear in strict sequence; they appear and reappear from different angles and vantage points. In doing so, further context and richness is added to the scenery. This seems to be a more accurate description of what happens. For instance, when we are in the connecting phase, we may experience new triggers that again create feelings of disintegration and despair. Also, as we start to integrate our experiences and gain greater understanding, we may find ourselves testing the boundaries and meeting our control issues again. In fact, it seems that we ricochet about the stages in a general forward direction rather than move smoothly through the process, one stage at a time.

However messy it becomes, this integrating stage brings an emerging sense of order that begins to reveal our Self; our true identity. It is as if something has been found that makes us feel more complete, more whole.

Heather said that she felt that what people now saw was the 'real me', whereas before, she thought they were only seeing a part of her; the part that she thought they wanted to see. Indeed, she expressed this stage as 'the inside joining the outside', conveying the sense that the more vulnerable side of her, the side of her that she had protected and hidden from view, was now what people saw.

When we contemplate controlling our boundaries, we often find that there are two impossibilities that struggle to co-exist; vulnerability and strength, fear and courage, control and recklessness. It would seem that the impossibilities of paradox, dichotomy or contradictions in term, embed themselves in the personality at the integrating stage. We are 'both/and' not 'neither/nor'. We are both vulnerable and strong. Frightened and brave. Controlled and reckless. For us, at this stage in our process, we are not held in the one dimensional, polar world. We are complex beings who can straddle the uncomfortable divide between extremes. And we have reached the point where we do not think this is inconsistent or surprising. It merely exhibits the texture and breadth of our personality and the complexity of our emotional and intellectual landscape.

At this point, you are probably able to live with your doubts and fears and ease away from the need for certainty, resolution or closure. You can hold the dichotomy softly and allow it to work itself out in its own time, or just live with it, present and perfect. Perhaps this notion can be best understood by thinking of going up in a helicopter to look down on yourself from a great height. You have moved away from the detail of the hand that does, the mouth that speaks, the foot that treads and you are able to see the complex workings of the whole of your body which can do, speak and move all at the same time. Then, even higher, and you begin to see how you interact with others and how this shared world can be so different in the realities of each person. Higher again and you see how people interact with their landscapes and yet higher again and you see how the different landscapes are juxtaposed. Sea against land. Desert against mountain. Forest against city. All the opposites co-existing. This is a representation of us too. We embody the opposites of air and water, flesh and bone, mind and matter, thought and emotion, right and wrong, beautiful and ugly, resignation and intention. We are a kaleidoscope of changing colours, patterns and form. We are an integrated whole; an authentic, inconsistent human being that makes complete sense and complete non-sense!

Integrating then seems to involve the ability hold two or more truths at once. As wider understanding is gained we actually consider opposites to be part of our whole truth. Unfortunately, the recognition of ourselves in these moments and the sense that it makes will probably only be fleeting. Very often we feel as if we have seen something vitally important only to find that it has been snatched away from us before we have fully captured it. Actually, our integrating will probably never make *complete* sense to us because it will be continually happening. We probably won't be able to talk about it lucidly or share its detail with anyone else but at least we will be able to convey the *feeling* of sense and sanity that it gives us! At least we begin to see the elephant! By drawing a wider circle around our meaning we are able to create the space for what was previously unthinkable. This enables us to move beyond our current reality and weave still further richness into our overall understanding and expectation of life.

Transformation relies on deep and courageous self-reflection. This leads to the deconstruction and reconstruction of meaning, which now includes and integrates more of our experience. In the elaboration and enlargement of the patterns of meaning we hold, we view the world differently. This new and wider worldview provides us with the foundation for greater understanding, wisdom and tolerance. We are less likely to make harsh judgements. There is always another side; an extenuating circumstance to be considered. It is the place where 'forgiveness' can enter the journey because you will now understand the unpalatable truth that it is possible to be both a perpetrator and a victim.

When I use the term 'forgiveness', I do so with caution. I do not see forgiveness as a sentimental, sugar-coated act that denies what's happened in the past or the culpability of the person whose behaviour was harmful. Nor is forgiveness a means of maintaining constant mind-over-matter vigilance that keeps memories and resentments at bay. It is more like an energetic severance from the investment in anger, pain or shame. Indeed, it might be argued that forgiveness is everything to do with the person who is doing the forgiving and nothing to do with the person who is being forgiven.

In the western culture in which I live, it seems that we are seduced into putting on 'you've done something wrong' spectacles when someone has affronted us or transgressed a law of some sort. When we don these spectacles, we effectively view people through lenses that have been tinted by their misdemeanours. So whatever they do, we see them in this light, never letting them forget it and never letting us forget it either. Through the permanence of our looking glasses, we cast a judgement and create a stigma that they are compelled to carry as long as we keep them in our view. But if we could see ourselves, we may notice that we look ugly in our glasses. Our behaviours are determined by our worldview and when we see it in such a jaundiced way, we may become guarded at best, unkind or vengeful at worst. Not only that, but we may share our perceptions with others and, when we do this, they might put on copycat glasses, glad to have a justification for their negative feelings. And soon, we'll have a massive pair of collective glasses that prevents any forgiveness or movement at all.

Although it may be an uncomfortable truth, the continual return to horrible memories through anger and resentment only succeeds in perpetuating those memories, it does nothing to change them. In energising the connection between now and the past, old images and feelings are drawn into the present. What happened may be in the distant past but the reality of it is being revitalised, re-experienced and held like a mirror only a few inches from our faces. This is not so much about 'forgiveness' then, it is about release. Once the 'mirror' has gone, so too has the reflection of the past. What lies ahead is fertile territory and a place in which to enjoy freedom and to exercise choice. Un-forgiveness indicates an energetic investment in the past, one that calls back people and situations that cause pain. It is only when this investment disappears and the need to forgive evaporates that the desired effect of forgiveness can occur. Forgiveness also paves the way for the next stage of the transformative process that brings such freedom and joy.

What I was surprised to notice in this study was that forgiveness did not emerge as a dominant theme. Indeed, often the women's commentary indicated that they felt no need or desire to forgive. They had moved on. The past exerted no pull on them any more.

The other surprising outcome from the conversations I had with the women was that in every case, their abuser had become old, diseased or senile before his time. My abuser died aged 21. He was riddled with cancer. Perhaps there is some satisfaction in the idea that these people had their 'karmic comeuppance' and finally reaped the seeds of their own destruction. I wonder... If an adult perpetrates violence against a child, does the toxicity that is first projected outward, later turn inward to poison the body of its host?

Saving graces: Integrating

It isn't until you come to a spiritual understanding of *who you are* – not necessarily a religious feeling, but the spirit within – that you can begin to take control.

The integrating phase is often quite reflective. It is a time when all the pieces of the puzzle are brought together to form an overall picture. It is also a time when the meaning of your life may be up for scrutiny. Who are you? Why are you here? What is it all for? What is to become of you in the grand scheme of things? Many women take the opportunity to explore different philosophical or spiritual traditions to give their lives meaning and to put them into a wider perspective. There's always meaning beyond meaning. It never stops.

Find a philosophical framework

You may find it helpful to identify a framework that puts words to your experiences. Sometimes, we feel so at sea that we don't even know how to give voice to our thoughts and feelings so exploring different philo-sophical, spiritual or religious frameworks may be helpful to you in doing this. If you are interested in taking your exploration beyond the Self and into this realm you may want to peruse a more extensive and learned resource. Whichever path you take, you are likely to be rewarded by awesome concepts that aim to answer 'meaning of life' questions. These questions have been posed for millennia and it is fascinating territory. For the purposes of your immediate journey, though, try to remember to keep things relevant to you in the present and helpful in the way you make meaning in your everyday life.

There are lots of introductory books that give you a quick glimpse into the different traditions which will help orientate you towards something with which you have a natural sympathy. Indeed, you may have stumbled across an enticing philosophical framework on your journey already. If you've taken up yoga or meditation, you may well have ventured into some of the Eastern spiritual philosophies which are rich with the impulse for life and growth. The martial arts also bring with them a tradition that can be tirelessly explored. However, you may want to delve into some of the more formal texts to see which religious and/or spiritual frameworks resonate with you. Whatever you do, remember to lead with your heart.

Release yourself from the pain

If you are having difficulty severing from your pain, you may like to try a technique called '*Cutting the ties that bind*' which is also the name of a book by Phyllis Krystal.[4] Doreen Virtue advocates the use of similar techniques in her book *The Lightworker's Way*.[5]

The 'ties that bind' are those virtual cords or 'telephone lines' that connect us psychically to the people that brought us pain. The more intense the relationship, the thicker are the connecting chords. And, the more you invest in that relationship, the thicker and more draining the cords become. The technique uses visualisation to bring to your mind images of the people who are at the other end of the cords and sapping your reserves. If you can visualise this scene, it will be easy for you to conjure up a large pair of very sharp scissors and observe yourself cutting the cords one by one. See them drop away and send a packet of compassion to the person at the other end every time you make a cut. You may also want to seal your end with white light. Inwardly ask for protection for you and the people you have 'cut away' so that you are both free to manage your boundaries more effectively and maintain energy and focus on your own business. If you have not done any visualisation work before, don't worry, just holding the intention and concentrating on the process will enable you to be just as effective as someone who is practised in this art. People often sense what they describe as a change in atmospheric pressure after completing this technique and report feeling much lighter and happier.

Staying with the topic of subtle energy, Eckhart Tolle[6] presents the notion of a 'pain-body'. The 'pain-body' is the receptacle for all accumulated pain and, when we invest in the pain of our past, the 'pain-body' is energised and it increases in size. The bigger it gets, the more pain it needs to feed itself and so it continually seeks sustenance from painful memories, situations and relationships. The pain-body contains the naive meaning that you have woven in order to cope with your childhood experiences but it is these experiences, along with inherited family susceptibilities, that lock you into further pain creation and perpetuation. The 'pain-body' is an illusion of the mind, which has been created by the ego as it fights, in a futile attempt to gain control of life. And, as the ego inevitably encounters obstacles and set-backs in its attempts, the 'pain-body' is created to accommodate the bruises and pain to the ego, which is now locked in battle with life. Indeed, the 'pain-body' begins to take on a reality of its own and orchestrates negative drama to justify its own existence. If, as adults, we recall and invest in the pain of our past and if we then expect pain and unhappiness to continue into our future, our lives will be filled with pain. Indeed, we will be locked into a vicious cycle, recalling, attending to and creating pain.

Although Emma did not use the concept of the 'pain-body', she nonetheless related how anger had kept her pain alive. She talked of being held in a dilemma that recognised the need to release her pain from the past but prevented her from actually doing it in the present. However, she did talk of softening her judgement and feeling more empathy towards herself in the present and the past. This compassion assisted her in the integrating process, where duality, the holding of two opposing thoughts, is accommodated. In this way, she could both acknowledge the pain and let it go; both/and.

Eckhart Tolle advocates observing or putting attention on the pain-body and deliberately diminishing the energy that is given to it so that it eventually shrinks and disappears altogether. It means attending to what is in the present only. Living in the 'now', tapping in to the 'power of now'.

Again, drawing on the wisdom of the Buddhist teacher Thich Nhat Hanh:

'Everyone walks on the earth, but there are those who walk like slaves with no freedom at all. They are sucked in by the future or by the past and they are not capable of dwelling in the here and now where life is available. If we get caught up in our worries, our despair, our regrets about the past and our fears of the future in our everyday lives, we are not free people. We are not capable of establishing ourselves in the here and now.... If we keep running away into the (past or) future, we cannot be in touch with the many wonders of life – we cannot be in the present moment where there is healing, transformation and joy.'

See things differently

You may have heard about 'The Work', a therapeutic process devised by Byron Katie to help people see and experience the part they play in perpetuating the effects of their own history. It rests on four probing questions that call us to examine 'the truth' about our sense of Self as a victim. She asks the person who she is working with to make a statement about something they believe to be true. This may be something like: "My father doesn't love me." She then gets them to examine the truth of this statement by asking four questions. They are: 1. Is it true? 2. Can you absolutely know that it's true? 3. How do you react when you think that thought? and 4. Who would you be without the thought? After this comes the 'Turnaround'. Turnarounds are opportunities to experience the opposite of your original statement and see what you and the one you have judged have in common. In this instance, it might be "I don't love me." The answers to the four questions, along with the 'turnaround' inevitably lead us to an understanding and acceptance of how we judge ourselves, and others. It is, Byron Katie says, through holding on to our judgements, or our indignation, that we continually re-experience our past pain. The four questions enable us to enter a process of enquiry into our thinking and give us the choice to stop colluding in the perpetuation of our pain. The process is rapid and often results in enlightened under-standing in a few minutes. You can learn about this process in Byron

Katie's book Loving What Is or by visiting her website: http://www.thework.com/ Some people believe that The Work takes us beyond forgiveness to a place where there is nothing and no-one to forgive.

STAGE 7 - TRANSCENDING

The word enlightenment conjures up the idea of some superhuman accomplishment, and the ego likes to keep it that way, but it is simply your natural state of felt oneness with Being. It is a state of connectedness with something immeasurable and indestructible, something that, almost paradoxically, is essentially you and yet is much greater than you. It is finding your true nature beyond name and form.

The Mermaid, Ed Org   **Eckhart Tolle**

I loved this image the minute I saw it. The mermaid appears to be in her truth, unabashed and unrepentant. She is open, beautiful, wide-eyed and focused on the horizon ahead. She brings together the air (her breath) and water (the ocean); both fluid, flowing life carrying forces that constantly move and change. She embraces the physical (the body) which uses the elements to give her grace, purpose and direction. She is enigmatic in her femaleness; sensual and sexual, fully integrated and fully detached.

Shake the dust from your shoes and move out of the shadows of the past, turn 180 degrees and face forward. This is what the final stage is all about. It is a highly optimistic stage where you can gather together all the pieces of yourself and draw from their collective strength to project your authenticity and uniqueness into the world.

Although transcending is the final stage in the transformative process, we know it has no finality. You have arrived at a sense of wholeness; you have found your true essence and you can recognise the many different aspects of yourself, but there is more to come. A friend of mine uses the analogy of the meniscus; that bulging dome of liquid that is trying to hold more volume than is available to it in its container. You have seen the effect when you fill a glass of water too full, when you measure too much olive oil onto a spoon or when you fill a vase before placing the flowers in it, only to find that they raise the level to overflowing as their stems are added. You are like a meniscus now, you have filled and exceeded your own capacity and there is growth and a new world ahead. When the meniscus is strained to its limit, it is minutes from its next expression; a bursting, flowing, rushing river that is seeking a new path and direction. The energy that was contained when the meniscus was at its fullest extent almost explodes with purpose as it is released to find its new place. Sometimes it moves so fast that we have to jump away from the liquid as it splashes onto the surface and seeks the edge. When the meniscus has broken through its skin, it can never be put back inside again, just as you are now too big to go back to the kind of containment that held you before. You have expanded. You have grown into the next level of your potential, and there is more to come. But for now, this is a time for celebration, a time to rejoice in yourself and in your achievements. You have travelled a long path and you can look back and see the route stretching out behind you. There is no need to go back there again. You are free to turn and put your sights on a new horizon.

This is the stage of letting go and letting be. It is the stage where you transcend the limitations that you have imposed upon yourself and it is where you embrace and express more of who you are. The women in this study talked of leaving behind the 'old me' and enjoying the 'new me' in all her fullness.

Heather made this part of the process particularly clear when she said that she started to be able to let it all go. 'Like letting go of a heavy weight. Like just casting a bit off at a time. Each little bit that I accepted and let go meant that I could take another step forward. I was slowing lightening my own load and then I found that I wasn't weighed down by everything any more. I was separate from it at last.'

Others talked of not associating with who they were as a child or feeling almost as if their history didn't happen. One woman spoke of feeling that she was carrying someone else's memories that were accessible but not powerful. When the women talked at this stage, they were not particularly emotional, but they were certainly moved. It is clear that the comments have a very different tone to that of 'denial'. There is acceptance yet there is distance. Equally, these comments are not infused with anger, guilt or shame. These emotions seem to have no place in the lives of these women now. Instead, there is a 'letting go', not in the sense of a descent into chaos, but in the sense of cutting the ties to a memory and demolishing its power to call them back into pain.

The final stage of this process gave the women the freedom to express themselves without neurosis, restriction or dependency. They were now free to explore their place in the world without intrusion from the past. They seemed to have arrived at, and had fully embraced, their womanhood. They were not afraid of their sexuality, sensuality, creativity or power. Their vitality and enthusiasm for the next stage of their life was almost palpable and the positive energy that emanated from them was inspirational.

Saving graces: Transcending

'It is never too late to become what you might have been.'

George Eliot

Be joyous

The saving grace on arriving at this part of the transformative process is the gift of confidence, optimism, happiness and joy. It is a place of total release from all potentially damaging or distracting connections with the past. It is a place of freedom and full self-expression.

Why don't you try something you've never done before but have always wanted to do? Take yourself for a picnic, to see a show or to browse around the shops. Indulge yourself with cups of coffee in bijoux cafés overlooking a river or by a canal. Spread the papers over your bed on a Sunday morning and add warm toast and a cup of tea to the experience. Lie naked in the garden under a full moon. Learn to dance.

Build new relationships

The rewards of having been through the process were many. Often new relationships had entered the lives of the women. Sometimes they had embarked upon new careers and above all, they carried a new sense of purpose.

You might like to use your new-found confidence to build different networks of friends or professional acquaintances. Now that you have an inner glow, you will find that others like you will be drawn to you. New people will start to appear in your life who may take you on another journey of discovery. Be discerning though, guard against those who want to steal your energy and power. You have now got what they want.

Explore your femaleness fully

Women that arrive at this place glory in their womanhood. Intimacy is not threatening to them now because their boundaries are managed effectively. They are free to explore their sensuality, sexuality and indulge in pleasures that have felt too threatening in the past.

Take yourself to a health spa and try body therapies, massage and facials. Have a mud wrap, chocolate wrap or a flotation. Use the Jacuzzi, sauna, steam-room, hydrotherapy pool or take a tropical effects shower, complete with thunder sounds and lightening strikes. Take a friend with you. Laugh uproariously. Have a make-up consultation, a manicure, a pedicure. Commission a 'personal shopper' to find a new style for you. This could be a good friend or a professional in a department store. Change your hairstyle, perhaps light instead of dark, and allow your femininity to express itself in full consciousness, not in self-consciousness.

Live in the present

Pain can no longer call you back into despair. You have released your pain, anger and shame through attending to and mastering the mind's insistent pull towards the past. Live life consciously and in the present. Give recognition to the fact that you are writing you own life script now; you are self-determined, not determined by some external force.

Take a holiday!

This is the time to rejoice in the release of your true nature. There is more to come. Be thankful for each emergence, for each blossoming. Feel the sun on your skin. Eat well. Relax!

Healing and transformation

> I am a woman in process. I'm just trying like everybody else. I try to take every conflict, every experience, and learn from it. Life is never dull.
>
> *Oprah Winfrey*

I have spoken a great deal about the process of transformation and I have related it to the journeys that the women described to me. However, it was not clear at the outset that they had been through a transformative process; clarity about this had to be found through their stories. Whilst listening to them, I was constantly looking out for a theme that would explain what had gone on in their lives; something that would make sense of all their experiences.

I could see that the process being described was one that involved reflecting, learning, interpreting and creating meaning and that it bore a strong resemblance to the natural growing and dying pangs that we experience in life. I was aware too, that as well as being a psychological process, it had an ephemeral quality to it; it was not just driven by the mind, but by the emotions, the body and the spirit. Indeed, some of the women explicitly shared their belief that their journey was somehow *meant to be*. It was part of their purpose or destiny. This belief was not distilled from logic, because in matters of hurt and pain logic doesn't come into it, but was born of a more philosophical orientation or faith. Sometimes they made sense of their experience in the context of a God but mostly they related their experiences to something that was 'bigger' than them. This did not negate their own qualities of courage, tenacity and compassion, nor did it factor out the need for intelligent reflection and deep thought. These qualities merely added to the attributes that facili-tated their journey.

During our conversations, each woman looked back over her experience and described the episode in her life that encompassed her process of change. It began when she recognised that her coping strategies were not working, it continued with her fall into 'chaos' and it proceeded with periods of deep consideration, the challenging of old assumptions and the recreation of meaning. Finally, she exercised choice and released more of her potential as well as revealed more of her authenticity. The expansion of her personality and the transparency of her truth seemed to come hand in hand.

'Healing', 'learning' and 'becoming' are all words that imply perpetual motion. They are generative, dynamic and fluid. Indeed, they are 'process' words that conjure up images of purposeful intelligent movement. Each time we enter the transformative process, we learn to recognise the next layer of assumptions, let them go, see what's left and move on. Slowly, as we learn to be more fluid with our thinking and more open to possibility and contradiction, we realise that it was our old thought patterns that created the prisons that contained us. We so strongly believed what we believed, that we were locked in and unable to escape our own cages, even though they were causing us pain. You can easily see that what we hold to be true becomes true. If we believe we are unlovable, we behave as if this was so and people find us unlovable. If we believe we are a failure, we behave as if this was so and we become a failure. We fulfil our own prophesies. When we recognise that our thoughts are illusions, that they are merely intellectual constructs that create the virtual bars of our cages, then we can find the power to move from being stuck to being free.

Although I have described the process in stages, again I stress that this is a simplification. Every pass has its own pattern of one step forward, two steps back, two steps forward, one step back. But whether it feels like it or not, we can be sure that the process is progressive, expansive and liberating. It also becomes familiar. This doesn't necessarily make it easier, but it does allow you to recognise what resources you need to help you move through the stages as swiftly as possible. And the meaning deepens each time. You are not just skating around on the surface, you are entering deeper understanding, and acquiring greater wisdom and releasing more of your potential each time you enter the process.

When there is no route map the journey can be very bewildering. Without the blueprint, the stages can appear to be temporary or permanent, random or planned, minor or overwhelming. In any of these conditions, it can be frightening to enter a new stage because you just don't know how much you're going to have to bear or for how long you're going to have to bear it. Many of the women said that if they'd had a route map, their hope may have been preserved a little longer – although there is no foregone conclusion that everything will be all right. Indeed, it would seem that there are times of silence and immobility when there is no apparent guarantee of further progress. Regardless of this, you can be sure that this is a process that does happen, whatever, and it has sufficient wisdom and integrity to unfold in the most helpful and effective way.

And it is a process that brings healing; it brings healing to old wounds, it brings healing to a broken spirit and it brings healing to the internal dilemmas that make life hard and uncomfortable. Healing and transformation, they come as a package.

Peaks, troughs and spirals

I have given a shape to the process of becoming. This came out of the descriptions given to me and the metaphors and words that were used. The women described a feeling of falling off the edge as they entered the disintegrating stage. They said that they had a sense that they were falling apart, that things were coming undone and that they were unable to hold it all together any more. At the outset, there is a real sense of an edge, like a cliff edge, over which you fall as your process takes you away with it.

At some point, the descent seemed to bottom-out and a sense of uncomfortable containment was experienced. This seemed to be a relatively static place for quite a period of time and was often described as the pit of despair, the abyss or the black hole. It has also been described as the dark night of the soul. Although this sounds dreadful, it really is a necessary process of undoing that later allows movement and freedom.

Try not to focus on this as if it was a negative stage, even if it feels like it. Once you've done the work, it's not long before the more positive energy sweeps in and takes you in an upward direction to the next stage. Integrating and the stages around it were often described as a bit of a climb, but steady and upward nevertheless. There was a much more positive air about this part of the process, like clearing out a wardrobe of old clothes. Previous thoughts were being reviewed, discarded, sorted, filtered and eventually a sense of clarity was achieved. It is hard work but there is always a great sense of satisfaction when it is finished.

When I was listening to the stories, it was at the final stage that I got such a sense of relief and release. The women glowed as they remembered the feeling of triumph. It really was worth it and the confidence and beauty that emanated from them would recommend the value of the process to anyone. Not only this, but they placed the transcending shape, their 'peak' perhaps, some distance above their starting point. They gained a new perspective; they reached a higher plane or achieved the pinnacle of success. Often it happened distinctively too. There was a moment when they realised that there was no going back, where they saw themselves doing something differently to the past and recognised that they were harvesting the fruits of their labours.

This curve is not a random structure presented for convenience; it was actually created by the women. Please refer again to the diagram shown overleaf.

The Hero's journey

Many of us are familiar with the notion of a journey through myths, legends and fairytales. But these are more than just stories, they symbolise the journey through life and reveal the patterns and challenges that are likely to befall us. So, as we take life's journey, we are bound to travel through hostile lands where we are stripped of our skills and talents. We are bound to be given tricky puzzles to solve and to meet people who are not what they seem. We are bound to encounter hideous

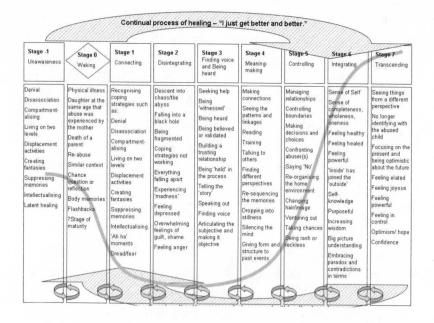

A Woman's Way – The seven stage transformative journey from hurt to happiness

beasts that we have to outwit or slay. Metaphorically speaking, if we are living, we are journeying. This is perhaps why we are here, on this spinning globe. So, let's assume that this is true, that we really are here to journey; that we are here to learn and grow in wisdom and to experience life and ourselves fully. And, as the peaks of life's experience are joyous, let us also assume too that we are here to experience that joy.

My aim in writing this book was to provide you with a kaleidoscope of information and ideas that would help you recognise and face the challenges of your own journey. In addition, I hoped to provide you with some tools to give you assistance in discovering everything you are, and to becoming a walking expression of your own truth. For these reasons, and to help you scale the peaks of wisdom and joy, I'd like to present you with another way of looking at the journey; that of the Hero's journey. Obviously, at first sight, this is a male journey and you may ask what relevance it has to women. However, I believe there are characteristics and stages of the Hero's journey that we can learn from and because of our femaleness; we can use these to illuminate our path further.

Let me guide you through the dynamics of the mythological journey; the Hero's journey.

According to Joseph Campbell[7], the point of the Hero's journey is to 'unlock and release the flow of life into the body of the world.' This implies that the Hero's journey, or the Heroine's journey in our case, is not just for the person undertaking it, but for the wider community. The challenges and disappointments are experienced not just for us, but for others. It is an act of service. Although we may feel isolated and alone on our journey, many have trodden the path before us and they have left clues, insights and gifts along the way. Together, these provide the resources for those of us who otherwise might feel lost and lonely.

The Hero's journey is a rite of passage which represents the various transformations from babyhood to infancy; from infancy to adolescence; from adolescence to adulthood; from adulthood to the wise man or woman and onward to our dotage. It is the process of realising (literally, bringing to reality) *who we are* and it is through meeting ourselves in this way that we find our connection to the world. What's more, it is through this connection that we are able to return, along with all our gifts and inspirations, to be of service. We literally become our own offering.

Needless to say, at the end of our journey, we are not the same person that we were at the beginning, we have transformed. In fairytales, this is usually signalled by the 'happy ever after' ending which often involves a Prince and a poor but beautiful and misunderstood girl. Cinderella comes to mind, as does Snow White and the Seven Dwarfs, Beauty and the Beast, Goldilocks and the Three Bears and other classics. Equally, it could be the 'return of the King'; a theme frequently encountered in mythology or legend such as the tale of Odysseus's return to Ithaca or Tolkein's Lord of the Rings. Dante's Divine Comedy provides another example. The endings in these tales represent the Hero's arrival at a place of universal connectedness, which is tempered by wisdom and shaped by feelings of confidence, clarity and capability, as well as dignity and humility. Having travelled, it is important to recognise that it is not the world that has changed, but your *perception* of the world.

By recognising the stages of the Hero's journey, you will develop an understanding of the energy flows and undercurrents that you will encounter and this will help you recognise their importance to you. It will also allow you to pay attention to the recurrent themes and focus your activities in the most helpful way. The Hero's journey is generally considered to comprise three main stages: *Separation* – the 'call to adventure' or departure from the ordinary world; *Initiation* – the tests, trials and learning that must be undergone and the integration of new understanding; and *The Return* – re-entry to the ordinary world carrying a prize or gift. This gift may symbolise or be the elixir of life, the Holy Grail, a timely rescue, a spiritual message or enlightenment.

Like the process of transformation, the first stage in the Hero's journey is the waking stage; the trigger or 'call to adventure'. This is a call to experience unimaginable challenges and to take action for which there has been no preparation or prior experience. The call to adventure is a summons that is instinctively feared for, although great rewards are promised, it is inevitable that your vulnerabilities and fears will be exposed, examined and tested. At this stage of the journey you are called to cross the threshold from what is known to what is unknown. It is sometimes described as entering the void or falling into the abyss. To add insult to injury, as you set off, all the talents and skills that you have accumulated will be useless to you and you will be thrown onto your inner, as yet unknown, resources.

The call to adventure may be heard in different ways. It may be an accident or chance happening, it may bubble up from the well of your being or it may be disguised as an innocent pleasure or experience. Sometimes, it may not feel so much like a call but a nudge resulting from feelings of discontent, a vague notion that your life is out of balance or a sense that things are 'not quite right'.

Of course, you can ignore 'the call', but if you do, you are likely to be left with a gnawing feeling of disquiet. Even if you did not *consciously* ignore the call, the subconscious mind *knows* that an opportunity for growth has been missed so it creates underlying feelings of unease and unhappiness. What is more, from now on, you aren't really left alone and increasingly obvious calls are issued. So, although a choice is given, it would seem that there is no choice *really* because the consequence of *not choosing* is itself a kind of deterioration, equalled only by the deterioration you may feel when the journey begins in earnest and the first chaotic stage is reached.

The initial boundary over which the Hero steps is often characterised by darkness and powerful forces. It is uncharted and dangerous territory where the protective rules of the known world are absent. Relationships are untrustworthy, strange beings unleash their devious forces upon you and the topography of the landscape is hazardous. The passage over the threshold into the dark unknown symbolises self-annihilation. It demands that you let go of your attachment to the idea of rescue and launch yourself into the unknown, for this is the threshold where everything that was known is lost. Nothing is certain but uncertainty and illusion. Your assumptions and beliefs must be dissolved, remixed and restructured in the face of your new experience. Crossing the first threshold leads to chaos, fragmentation, self-doubt and often, despair.

If you obey the call however, you are given a wise guide or helper to assist you. More often than not, this is an unexpected meeting with someone who has just the right piece of knowledge to help you. Otherwise, you might recognise that someone you already know has held this valuable knowledge all along but you just didn't recognise it. There is an old saying: 'If the pupil is ready, the teacher will appear'. How reassuring this is when your needs are great! However, this teacher won't take the heat out of the situation for you. It is you that is journeying, not them. Their role is to drive you hard, throw you on your inner reserves and draw previously unmet talent from the soles of your boots. Although they will drive you hard, they will also act as a guide or mentor - and they do come with a tacit promise that the future will be brighter.

One of the most famous Hero's journeys, and one that I have alluded to several times in this book, is Dante's[8] journey through Hell and Purgatory to Paradise. Dante wrote The Divine Comedy in the fourteenth century. It describes his own journey from what we might call a mid-life crisis, to wholeness. At the outset of his poem, Dante is lost in a dark forest where his exit is barred by three beasts; a leopard, a lion and a she-wolf which, we gradually learn, represent his love of pleasure, his fierce pride and the greed and avarice of his ego. As he deliberates his escape, his guide and mentor, Virgil, appears and offers him the promise of freedom, albeit along a long and arduous path. However, it is this path that will equip him with self-knowledge and wisdom, and it will do so by introducing him to his shadow side.

Dante's call was triggered by the stage in life that he had reached; his mid-life. It manifested as a natural but increasingly determined sense of unease until it reached a point where he felt that he *had* to take the journey. His companion, Virgil, was characterised as a wise man and a friend yet in truth, Virgil was Dante's inner voice or his higher self.

In this life, and as Dante recognises, we often need to hear our thoughts in order to recognise what they are. Trying to work things out in our head is really difficult. It is generally much easier if we are able to speak them out and have them reflected back to us. Then we can know how we feel about them and whether or not they really do represent what we think. The role of the counsellor, therefore, is a crucial one in helping us do this. She will help us speak out what's in our minds by asking us some good questions. In responding to her, we will hear our thoughts, be able to judge them and then integrate them. In reality, we may need more than one person to perform this function for us as sometimes, we discover new territory which needs a different pair of ears. In Dante's case, Virgil performs this service as he accompanies him to the gates of Paradise. It is here that he is replaced by Dante's former earthly love, Beatrice, who takes over the task of bringing him into enlightenment.

Having crossed the threshold into the unknown, we move into a place of fluidity where there is 'no form'. Strangely, it is in this place of 'no form' that we encounter 'form' in the way of blocks, barriers and obstacles, the successful negotiation of which allows you to progress to the next stage. It's perhaps a bit like encountering rocks and boulders as we are carried down a river by its flow. Both ironically and inevitably, the particular obstacles that we face are certain to test us in those areas where we have the least skill or knowledge and where we are at our most vulnerable. However, it seems that profound learning comes from moments like these and it is, perhaps, precisely because we are forced to face our fears and weaknesses, that we are able to integrate our experience and create new meaning. The revelations that we have as a result of being buffeted about in the water, therefore, help us to move closer and closer to who we are, *really*.

Vivid dreams are often a feature of this stage of the process. Perhaps it is because we are trying to sort out so much that is new to us, that we need the assistance of the subconscious mind. Through images and symbols, dreams bring to mind the processing that is being done out of consciousness. This enables us to access and understand more of what is going on and bring it to the concrete world where it can be dealt with more objectively.

Dreams of passing down endless narrowing corridors or of squeezing oneself into tiny rooms were commonplace amongst the women in the study who could remember their dreams. Perhaps they signify the metamorphosis – or transformation - that defines this part of the adventure. Symbolically, these dreams may represent the neck of the womb through which the first metamorphosis of life takes place. At this stage in the Hero's journey, it is said that we die to the old ego in order to birth the new.

We have seen that one of the many coping strategies used by the women in the study was intellectualisation; an activity that kept them 'safely' in the head and protected them from identifying with their feelings. Unfortunately, not only did this strategy prevent them from recalling their feelings, but also from having any feelings at all! There is a real issue, therefore, with staying in the head and, as a result of society promoting reason and intellect over instinct and intuition, we often go there thinking that it will serve our purposes. However, all it does is create a kind of sterility that rids us of the richness of feeling. As women, we can match anyone intellectually, but we can only add our uniqueness if we are also docked with our feelings.

The next stage in the Hero's journey is named 'meeting with the Goddess'. Not only does the Goddess have all the virtues of a 'good' woman; the comforter, the healer, the friend, the lover, the nurturer, but she also has the qualities of a 'bad' woman; the forbidding, the punishing, the remote and the dangerous. The Goddess unites both the 'good' and the 'bad' of woman, therefore, and elevates these beyond the personal to the universal level. She is the universal mother, wholehearted and authentic in all she is. She is free from others' projections and expectations and transmits only her truth into the world. She is the totality of what can be known and, in our case, she is the one who comes to *know herself*. So, this stage, for the Heroine's amongst us, might be termed 'finding the Goddess within'.

If the Hero has a meeting with the Goddess who exemplifies the best mix of female attributes, then we might also consider the Heroine meeting with the God who exemplifies the best mix of male attributes. In the past thirty or forty years, women have switched from playing men at their own game to integrating some of the male qualities that enable them to more fully express themselves. Although largely considered to be the male preserve in the past, self-determination, autonomy, power and strength are amongst the virtues that are now found in women. We have a long way to go though. The dominance of male values throughout the centuries has had a devastating effect on women.

Whether you subscribe to meeting the opposite qualities in your encounter or not, this stage of the journey is designed to bring forth and integrate the animus with the anima. So, whatever gender you are, or whatever sexual persuasion you have, you will be exploring those aspects of yourself that are complementary to your dominant expression.

Atonement (at-one-ment) requires that attachment to the ego is abandoned so that we are free to feel at one. It is the ego that is affronted when we are hurt and this often leads us to want an apology, revenge or punishment. By placing attention on this 'unfinished business', we are focusing on the other and this means we can only be less of ourselves. This focus must be withdrawn if we are to be fully revealed.

At-one-ment is clearly an important stage on the Hero's journey and one that is often confused with forgiveness. But we must be clear what it actually means here. This is not so much about forgiveness in its common form; it is much more about bringing oneself into wholeness by detaching from other people's past thoughts and actions. If you imagine a bucket with tiny holes in it trying to contain water, you will perhaps get a sense of what it means to allow your energy to be drained by attachment to another person. At-one-ment is like plugging all the holes so that you can feel whole, complete or contained – or at one.

In Eric Fromm's book, *The Art of Loving*, he recognises at-onement as the deepest need of man (or woman). As he explores this in greater depth, he suggests that the ability to attain at-onement depends on the level of individuation reached. Clearly an infant cannot attain at-onement when she is dependent upon her mother's breasts for sustenance. However, as an adult, it can be (mimicked) through orgiastic states; whether they be trance induced or sexually induced. In such heightened (but transitory) states, 'the world outside disappears, and with it, the feeling of separateness from it.' (pp 11) Conformity and community also bring with them a *sense* of oneness, although it may be argued that they don't have the same intense allure as an orgasm! For this reason, conformity and community may not have the same persistent attraction as a sexual encounter. However, the urge for at-onement may explain why people seek others to make them feel whole, in spite of the fact that the emphasis on this part of the Hero's journey is not to look outside oneself for wholeness, but to experience it within.

The penultimate stage of the Hero's Journey is named 'Apotheosis', which means 'deification' or the elevation of a person to the rank of God or Goddess. In his book, *The Hero with a Thousand Faces*, Joseph Campbell defines the term apotheosis as 'the divine state which the human Hero attains who has gone beyond the last terrors of ignorance.' He qualifies this by saying: 'When the envelopment of consciousness has been annihilated, then he becomes free of all fear, beyond the reach of change.' This stage can be further described as non-dualistic. No longer do the polar opposites of male and female, good and bad, dark and light hold us in the world of duality. Instead, an integrated perspective is reached where such contradictions are held in balance.

Incidentally, Joseph Campbell told of the second ceremony of manhood which was conducted by the Murngin tribe in Australia; a tale which I think epitomises this stage of the journey. To mark the point at which dualistic thinking was transcended, a ceremony was conducted. It was designed to symbolise a state of uniformity, in the sense of 'one form', from the two gender expressions of human beings. This is how it happened. After a boy had passed through the ordeal of circumcision, he underwent a second ritual which signified the full integration of male and female. During this ritual, the underside of his penis was slit open to form a permanent cleft in the urethra. This formed the 'penis womb' or a male vagina, symbolising that he was now 'more than man'; fully integrated, male and female. Thankfully, the transformative healing journey holds no such trial for us, literally speaking, but figuratively, the essential step of integration does exist and is necessary if the transformative journey is to be completed.

Integrative thought and a sense of connection to a greater perspective naturally evaporates self-delusion and illusory thinking. Indeed, in the absence of our old thought constructs, we experience a sense of emptiness. When empty, our light can shine without casting shadows.

Rumi, a Sufi poet and mystic born in 1207, had something to say on the subject of Being Empty:

A Song of Being Empty
A certain Sufi tore his robe in grief,
and the tearing brought such relief,

He gave the robe the name faraji,
which means ripped open, or happiness,
or one who brings the joy of being opened.

It comes from the stem faraj, which also
refers to the genitals, male and female.

His teacher understood the purity
of the action, while others
just saw the ragged appearance.

If you want peace and purity,
tear away your coverings.

This is the purpose of emotion, to let
a streaming beauty flow through you.

Call it spirit, elixir, or the original
agreement between yourself and God.

Opening into that gives peace,
a song of being empty,
pure silence.

When we return from our Hero's journey, it is impossible to arrive back at the same place that we started from and carry on as we once did. Nothing feels the same anymore because we have left, and changed.

Many people, remote acquaintances, close friends and intimate lovers, will try to encourage you back into the expression of your old Self. This was the 'you' they knew and understood and they don't have the same understanding of who you are now. If this doesn't force them to question themselves, it forces them to question you, so you get the brunt of their confusion. This can sometimes mean that you have to leave old relationships behind. They just can't hold the complexity of you now. You are unfamiliar and uncomfortable to them.

Finally you enjoy the freedom to live fully. No longer are you attached to your personal limitations nor are your behaviours orchestrated by your past experiences. Perhaps you have begun to enjoy self-discovery and are keen to go on another journey. You are free to live spontaneously; to live the creative bliss of your becoming. You *are*.

Below, you will see the Hero's journey expressed from the female

Departure			Initiation			Return	
Waking	Connecting	Disintegrating	Finding voice and Being heard	Meaning-making	Controlling	Integrating	Transcending
Stage 0 The 'call to adventure'	**Stage 1** Crossing the outward threshold	**Stage 2** The road of trials	**Stage 3** The meeting with the Goddess	**Stage 4** At-one-ment (with the Father)	**Stage 5** Apotheosis	**Stage 6** Crossing the return threshold	**Stage 7** Freedom to Live
A call to leave the 'ordinary' world behind and awaken the Self. A crisis. A mistake. Serendipity or 'chance'. A bubbling discontent that emerges from the depths of the Self. An 'encounter' with a person who challenges you and raises your awareness about your fears and limitations.	Choosing to step over the threshold into darkness, danger and the unknown. Fear of self-annihilation – the 'inner' journey. A guide or wise person offers to accompany the Heroine on her journey. Temptation to deny the 'call to adventure' and ignore its impetus to travel into the 'underworld' or 'deep forests'.	Disintegration of what is known and the experience of 'no form'. Descent into the underworld. Exploration of the sub-conscious mind. Encountering and overcoming (metaphorical) daemons, ogres, serpents dragons and beasts. Letting go of the adherence to child-like expectations and anger at the parents or guardians. The ego is challenged and put to death. Who am I? Re-birth.	The emergence of 'womanhood'. Finding the Goddess, within. Holding the polarity of 'good' and 'bad' and expressing the Self genuinely and joyously. Being 'seen'. Being all-knowing. Exploring one's sexuality and embracing sensuality. Experimenting with being the 'temptress'.	Childlike expectations of the 'father' are readjusted and the nature of the relationship changes. Separation from an investment in 'hierarchical' relationships that were invested with expectation. Coming into 'selfhood' through abandoning the ego. At peace in the understanding of the 'revelation of Being'. Experiencing connectedness with the universe. Feeling a sense of at-one-ment with everything in the broadest terms.	Going beyond ignorance and the containment of consciousness. The release of personal potential. Integration: The perfect marrying of the feminine and masculine principles. The end of dualistic thinking and the beginning of connected thinking. All is one. Loss of self-delusion and illusory thinking. Seeing the Divine within. Emptiness.	The adventurer returns from the darkness to the world with her Majesty, the hard-won gift – elixir of life, The Holy Grail, wisdom, enlightenment. Conveying the experience of the adventure using recognisable and meaningful language and symbols. Explaining the unexplainable. Bringing back precious knowledge of the mystery and meaning of life.	The reconciliation of the individual consciousness with the universal will. Living without attachment to or investment in outcomes. Finding the essential Self. Living freely in the present. Finding peace and joy. Living in a state of Becoming without fear or the delusion of permanence. Knowing and allowing what *is*. The 'Awakened Self'.

The Heroine's Journey

perspective. It is now The Heroine's Journey. I have superimposed the stages from the transformative process on to the Hero's journey and rendered them relevant to the female traveller. I think you'll see a remarkable similarity between the two. However, there may be some differences in the detail of the overlap, most likely in respect of the need to find voice, be heard and be validated.

The journey through the chakras

In the current economic climate of the Western Hemisphere, our basic needs are more easily satiated than ever they were and we don't need to spend as much time in our search for food, shelter and entertainment. As a result, our attention has moved to different activities and our search for meaning has become a dominant theme. Collectively, we have picked our way through a range of philosophical and spiritual traditions that have challenged the paradigm and brought us close to ideas that were previously hidden, such as the more esoteric wisdom of the East. This groundswell of interest in Eastern philosophies has introduced esoteric practises to many enabling them to reach greater self-understanding and enrichment. If you are attracted to an examination of the major philosophies and religions, you may wish to seek seminars and programmes to attend or join discussion groups which are prepared to explore a wide range of beliefs without prejudice or coercion. However, there is one aspect of most major philosophies and religions, excluding perhaps atheism and existentialism, that provides a helpful framework for transformative healing. It is based on the belief that we not only have a physical body, but an energy body as well. It is sometimes referred to as the 'etheric' or spiritual body. In turn, this etheric body comprises a number of other bodies which are variously called the emotional body (feelings), the causal body (karmic), the mental body (mind) and the body of intuition (soul). The physical body is suffused by the etheric body which is anchored in place by the chakra system.

Although there are many interpretations of the number and function of the chakras, it is generally accepted that there are between five to seven main chakras holding the different 'subtle' (non-physical) bodies to the material (physical) body. The chakras are rooted in the physical body along the spinal column and are situated adjacent to the main nerve centres and endocrine glands. Their function is to pass life-sustaining energy or vitality (known as prana by the Hindus) and messages from the cosmos to the physical body in order to maintain its health. The efficiency with which they do this is dependent upon their state of health and the state of their health is, in turn, defined by the psychological, emotional and physical wellbeing of their host.

Chakra is the Sanskrit word for 'moving wheel' or disc and the chakras manifest as energy vortices, trumpets or funnels with the stem innermost and the 'flower-head' facing outward from the body. Each of the chakras vibrates at a different frequency and is associated with a different colour and set of qualities. Chakras can become 'grubby', damaged or blocked through accumulated negative experience. Emotional upsets, abuse, conflicts, fears and insecurities are common causes of damage that create illness or dis-ease.

The **root** chakra (located at the base of the spine) is red and connects you to the earth, your culture, your tribe and your sense of family. It is the human touchstone and relates to issues of survival, safety and security. Anger is also often held here; especially if it is within your family unit. Interestingly, anger is an emotion that is often perceived to be red. The root chakra is the foundation of mental, emotional and psychological health as all these are laid down through the family experience and early social influences. Fears of abandonment, of being unable to survive, stem from this chakra. The qualities of loyalty, justice and honour reside here because they belong to a structure; an accepted family, social or cultural structure in which the codes of practice, or rules of engagement, are accepted and respected. Damage at the root is common as most dysfunction begins at the family level; it also rocks the foundation on which the other chakras sit.

The **sacral** chakra (located in the abdomen, genital and lower back areas) is orange and represents sexual desires, self-acceptance and self-love as well as love of another. This is the chakra of relationship; it represents how you see yourself in the world, how you take care of yourself and how you relate to others. Our 'gut instincts' come from this energy centre too. Of course, not only is this chakra the harbour of our sexual desires, it is also the place where we hold our sexual traumas. As we emerge from our root, or tribal chakra, where the family or group is our identity, the sacral chakra is the place where we generate a sense of our own identity and create our psychological boundaries. It is where we encounter our first separation, from the unity of the family to self-definition in respect to, or in rejection of, the family. Fear of losing our autonomy, of losing our ability to make choices, sits in this location. This refers to our ability to provide for ourselves financially and materially. Fear of being controlled by another also resides here as it threatens our independence and prevents us from interpreting our own creativity.

The **solar plexus** chakra (situated just below the navel in the stomach area) vibrates to the colour yellow. Continuing the theme of separation, this is the chakra of personal power. It enables us to assert ourselves and separate from our inherited identity. It is where qualities such as self-esteem and self-confidence sit. It enables you to project yourself powerfully into the world through your ability to manage crises, take personal risks and display the courage of your convictions. No doubt you have heard the expression 'yellow-bellied' to describe someone who is weak and cowardly. These people are not taking responsibility for who they are; they shun their truth. This is the antithesis of the solar plexus chakra point. The occupation of self-discovery focuses on the solar plexus and brings it to health. Through self-discovery, we begin to understand why we do the things we do, what values and beliefs we hold and what importance we place on others' approval of us. Building this awareness equips us with what we need to make active choices instead of passive acceptances.

The **heart** chakra (superimposed on the heart area) is green and represents the means by which you make connections with others; how you connect with them through the heart. It is concerned with love and compassion. The heart centre is the middle chakra and it also brings together and integrates the many opposites such as male/female, head/heart, mind/body and persona/shadow. We can transmute our negative experiences, through compassion, and arrive at a place of healing, both for ourselves and others. Minimising one's attachment to others' motivations and actions allows us to continue the process of separation and find harmony and peace on an inner level as well as on the outer level. If we cannot let go, we may be racked by bitterness, anger, jealousy, resentment and hatred. All these are toxic and self-destructive emotions that sit in opposition to love and compassion. The only way to heal ourselves and others is to let these feelings go and choose to reside in a self-loving place where others' business is just that – theirs! Loving oneself means releasing the residue of damaging family or intimate relationships and choosing not to be the victim; a difficult challenge in a society where the victim is the subject of fascination and glorification.

The **throat** chakra (situated on the throat near the larynx) is blue and it concerns itself with the communication of our truth and the expression of our 'inner voice'. It is also responsible for how we see ourselves creatively and professionally and it enables us to speak within the boundaries of our own integrity, putting our self-knowledge and personal power behind the messages we send out into the world. This communication allows us to be seen and known for who we are for it reflects our attitudes and our beliefs. It is where we align ourselves authentically and congruently with all aspects of who we are. If our hearts are 'saying' one thing and our voice is saying another, our communications will not appear genuine. People will feel that something is not quite right; there is dissonance between what is said and what is meant. Our choices, then, are broadcast from our throat chakra for the world to hear and appraise. This is the chakra of coaching, teaching, guiding and advising. It is also the chakra of protest, when the scales are weighed too far against our own truth ideologically, politically, socially or behaviourally, we must attempt to redress the balance by 'speaking out' and making our choices transparent and unquestionable.

The **third eye or brow** chakra (positioned between the eyebrows) is indigo in colour and is responsible for how we 'see' from a logical, intuitive and psychic perspective. It is sometimes referred to as the site of second sight or the third eye. Not only is it where our intuition lies but it is also responsible for our logical thinking and reasoning abilities. This is where our ability to separate ourselves from our thoughts is seated so that we are able to reveal the patterns that exist in our minds and judge their viability. It is by using these perceptive qualities that we can view our meaning framework from a distance, look at the assumptions we hold and understand why and how we justify and support our behaviours. When we can do this dispassionately, we can decide whether or not we want to change those that are self-defeating and undermining what we want. It is here we are given the key to our own mysteries; our conscious and unconscious processes are revealed. Having arrived here, we are at last able to recognise the intricacies of our own intellectual workings and understand their power to construct meaning. So, from this point on, we can detach from our perceptions, live fully in the present and start being the arbiter of our own fortunes.

And finally, the **crown** chakra (situated on the top of your head) vibrates to all the colours and manifests variously as white, opalescent or violet-gold. It is often referred to as the many petalled lotus and it connects you to 'the Source'. It is the chakra of enlightenment, of spiritual connection and bliss. The crown chakra is often considered to be the channel through which spiritual messages and guidance are given and a sense of connectedness to the 'whole' is attained. This is where transcendent wisdom is gained and mystical connections are made. It is the place of 'holism'. It is the where the communication or recall of higher purpose takes place. The continued theme of increasing levels of separation from the tribe takes one to connection with the spiritual world and further detachment from the material world. As you connect with the Divine flow, infinite and unconditional compassion and love, pure and blissful joy can be experienced.

If you don't subscribe to the chakra system, you may nonetheless see that the transformative healing journey maps onto the movement from the base chakras to the higher chakras from a symbolic perspective. I have outlined the process using chakra language below.

The first stage of the transformative healing journey emerges from an acknowledgement that the rules and regulations laid down by your family in childhood no longer hold true. Referring back to the notion that none of us emerge from childhood emotionally unscathed, we all start here. As children, then, the foundations that were created for us contained our family's characteristic cracks and instabilities and it was onto these that our worldview was built. Although, as children, we don't question the integrity of the foundation explicitly, we may 'know' that it is different to others' foundations, so we keep it a secret and it becomes a taboo. As we grow, however, we experience 'the widening gyre' and an increasing feeling of inner discord until it reaches a point where it is impossible to hold the contradiction any longer. This may result in sadness, depression, obsessive/compulsive behaviours, self-harm or chemical dependency. It may also result in a series of 'bad' relationships.

Very often anger emerges from the cracks in the foundations and this needs to be expressed and exhausted before further work can be done. In fact, it appears from the study that if anger is not successfully vented, it prevents the healing process from taking place fully.

At this first stage of the healing journey through the chakras, issues of rejection and abandonment have also to be dealt with. Rachel, as you may remember, experienced abandonment when, as a seven year old child, her mother chose to keep her sister and put her into a foster home. This fear of abandonment, which was built into the foundations stones of her being, dogged Rachel throughout her adult years until she was able to address it in therapy and learn to rely on her own capabilities and self-love.

Any sexual damage in the sacral area commonly results in self-dislike or self-loathing and can lead to various forms of self-harm; an effect that frequently has to be worked through in the presence of a counsellor or therapist where it is safe to be seen and heard and where a feeling of legitimacy is gained. For Kate, she had to return to the basics and learn how to build and maintain a relationship before she could make any progress because this fundamental human skill had not been modelled for her as a child.

Financial security is considered to be a second chakra issue and is one that is commonly used as a controlling mechanism in dysfunctional relationships. Many women have vulnerabilities about being able to survive financially when they are not in a relationship and this can keep them tied to someone for years, especially if there are children to raise.

For those that have been abused as children your will and personal power, held in the navel centre, will have been thwarted and damaged. The right to take self-responsibility and the right to control your environment would have been denied you in your early years and this would have set up a pattern of apparent weakness and helplessness. Third chakra healing challenges concentrate, therefore, on developing self-understanding and re-capturing the means and courage to express yourself truthfully. Validation is very important to you at this stage of your healing journey. If it was not given to you as a child, you will probably need to find an environment in which you are witnessed, believed, validated and given approval.

As a result of being accepted and approved of, self-love and compassion for others begins to flow. I have already described the act of forgiveness from an energetic standpoint and you may remember that it can also be thought of as the removal of dependency on the pain-body; a notion explored by Ekhart Tolle. The release of pain is what concerns healing at the heart chakra. By merely observing the pain-body and recognising the damaging drain it imposes on your energy levels, it is possible to stop the dysfunctional courtship of pain. By removing attention from the pain-body and starving it of energy, it will no longer be able to dominate your life. Clarifying these dynamics, entering 'forgiveness', being in the heart, experiencing self-love and investing in personal growth is the business of this stage of the healing process. The act of forgiving, or disengaging from the impact of abusive people or memories, brings to an end the continual call back to our wounds so that they can no longer damage us.

Continuing to move up the chakras, a new creative energy and authority in the personal professional contexts represents arrival at the throat chakra. Having the confidence to speak your truth, command your world, put authority behind your choices, manage your boundaries and project yourself authentically into the world are all characterised by healing in the area of the throat chakra. Often the women chose to use their understanding and experience to assist others on the transformative journey of healing. They decided to share their truth so that others didn't feel alone and disorientated as they tried to make sense of their own transformative path.

As a result of the learning and transformation gained on their journey, the women established a new place in the world. Using their intuitive forces held in the area of the third eye, they were able to integrate all that they had experienced and learned. This enabled them to reach a new consciousness which they used to make decisions and take control of their lives.

Finally, arrival at the crown chakra brings feelings of enlightenment, joy or bliss. There is disassociation, not through disinterest or denial, but through a transcendent sense of moving beyond what was. This is the reward for undertaking the journey. It heralds a movement from personal falsehood to personal truth. This disassociated feeling can lead to a sense of connection with the Divine Source, the universal energy or God. It is as if you have raised your sights from the ground to the skies and, instead of being caught up in past troubles, you can look forward to rewarding connections with people and nature.

Below I have shown an interpretation of the transformative healing journey as a journey through the chakras, from the root to the crown. This journey has also been interpreted as a life stage journey in a recent book by Susan Wright called *Chakras in Shamanic Practice: Eight Stages of Healing and Transformation.*

If you subscribe to the above hypothesis, there are many chakra cleansing and balancing meditations available in texts, on CDs or on the web. You will find a very good one in Doreen Virtue's book *The Lightworker's Way* (1997: pp 189-192).

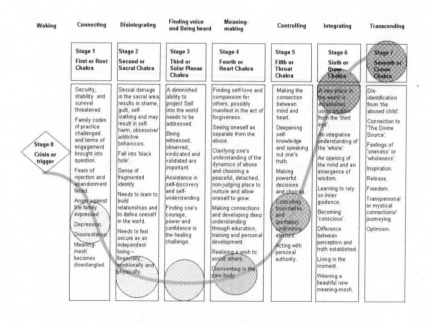

The journey through the chakras

Chakra Meditation

Using the visualisation techniques that you have already developed, form an image of your body in your mind's eye and visualise your chakra system as seven coloured spheres starting from the bottom of your spine and ascending along the spinal column to the top of your head.

As you begin the meditation, ask for protection and guidance and cloak yourself in white light.

Beginning with the root chakra, conjure up an image of a red ball, spinning and pulsating gently at the base of your spine. From a point at the centre of the ball, draw out a beam of white light and see it begin to infuse and brighten the ball. Continue to observe this light as it travels outward in all directions until the red ball appears to shine and shimmer brilliantly.

Moving up the body to the sacral chakra, conjure up an image of an orange ball, spinning and pulsating gently in your abdomen. From a point at the centre of the ball, draw out a beam of white light and see it begin to infuse and brighten the ball. Continue to observe this light as it travels outward in all directions until the orange ball appears to shine and shimmer brilliantly.

Envision each chakra in turn and cleanse it with the white light that emanates from the centre of the coloured ball. When you have worked through all your chakras and they are all clean, glowing and of equal size, seal your body in white light and give thanks for the cleansing.

Birth as a Metaphor

'Since the stars have fallen from heaven and our highest symbols have paled, a secret life holds sway in the unconscious. Our unconscious hides living water, spirit that has become nature, and that is why it is disturbed. Heaven has become for us the cosmic space of the physicists, and the divine empyrean (the highest heaven) a fair memory of things that once were. But the heart glows, and a secret unrest gnaws at the roots of our being.'

    C G Jung

Since the stars have fallen... a secret life holds sway... and Heaven holds a fair memory of things that once were. I saw the 'truth' of this quote from Jung through another experience given to me by Zoë-Hope which I'd like to offer you as a window into 'what is' – perhaps. This happened when she was just three. Maybe this was just in time; before she lost the memory of where her 'spirit that has become nature' was rooted. It was my birthday and my extended family had turned up to help me celebrate. We were eating pizza, drinking beer and having a really good time in the garden where we could enjoy the last of the summer light and warmth. I had put a ring of multicoloured fairy lights at the bottom of the garden to make the atmosphere pretty and I said to Zoë-Hope, "Let's go and sit in the fairy ring for a while." I thought she might like it being three and having been introduced to life's mysteries through fairy tales and Walt Disney fantasies. So we strolled down the garden hand in hand, just her and me, and sat in the fairy ring together. It was a bright night and the stars were out in their thousands. They hung low in the clean dark of the countryside where competing light from street lamps didn't detract from their brightness. I drew her attention to the sky and she looked up in wonder. Then she said "Look Grandma, that's my star." She was pointing to a very bright star and said again "That's my star!" I said, "I see it. Is that where you come from?" She said, "Yes, it's my star." Whereupon, her voice cracked and she began to cry. In fact, she became very distressed and started saying "It's going Grandma, my star is leaving me." I caught her distress and became tearful myself. She was panicking. Her star was leaving her. "No", I said "It's OK. It's not leaving you, it's twinkling. You see? It has come back again." She was not convinced, nor was she comforted, so we sat in that fairy ring together, crying. Was that the 'truth' that she had shared? The poignancy of that moment is hard to convey. The conviction and passion of a three year-old is so real and their truth is undeniable. I sometimes ask her where she comes from now that she is older. "Mummy's tummy, silly!" she says. What a shame children have to grow!

I started this book with the birth of Zoë-Hope, a profound trigger for my own process. I am ending this book with another tale of Zoë-Hope as she steps along the path of her own truth and finds the magic within her. Both moments are births; the first a physical birth, the second a birth in consciousness. It seems fitting, therefore, to close this book by exploring birth as a metaphor for the transformative journey.

All births carry the same dynamic, whether they be physical or spiritual. Before the waters break, or before the waking stage is experienced, the pregnancy advances out of sight and out of consciousness. The baby grows by itself without intervention or interference from the mother just as consciousness grows increasingly expectant of its birth into fullness. These are latent processes. They continue under their own steam and with their own wisdom until the pregnancy, or moment of awakening, reaches its full term. At this point baby, or realisation, is fully formed and they are able to take on their own lives. For the first time mother, there is no knowledge of what it will be like once the birth has taken place. In fact, it is quite scary to have to care for another human being without prior training or knowledge. It may feel like standing on the edge of the abyss and looking into the unknown.

When the waters break, or the waking moment is experienced, there is no going back. Control is lost and the process takes over. The breath quickens. The contractions are felt. The heart beats faster and the pain comes. Nothing can return the mother and baby to the pre-birth idyll, just as nothing can force realisation back to the pre-conscious state. Things are coming undone. This is like the chaotic stage in the process of transformation; the stage at which meaning is challenged. It is also the stage where all that was previously known, doesn't help in entering the unknown.

The birth process is commonly assisted by someone who can offer support and experience. In a physical birth, this is the midwife. In a spiritual birth, this is the counsellor, therapist or confidante. Whatever the nature of the birth, this person replaces the 'structure' that has been lost and acts as a guide in the birthing process and a witness to the birth. It is interesting that many women are accompanied by women as they go through this process. It is a rite of passage that is both solitary, yet witnessed and shared. It brings a sense of connection when all sense; all control, is lost. Women supporting women; is that not a fundamentally female phenomenon?

Before the birth, baby and mother were one, all was known. Now the baby and mother are separate. For the fist time mother, or for the person going through the transformative process for the first time, nothing is known. It is like entering a dark forest. When we face such a place, we have to talk about it, be heard, encouraged and validated. The mid-wife often performs this function. She witnesses us as we give birth and carries us through to the other side. The counsellor does the same when we enter the process to birth ourselves. Eventually, we reach a place of respite, a place where we can objectify, consider and integrate our experience. Two realties co-exist. Mother and baby are separate; breathing their own air, pumping their own blood. Subject (our experience) and object (the perceptions we have about our experience) are separate too; hidden truths have been brought into the light, exposed for scrutiny and sense-making. In this process, we separate from our ignorance; our embeddedness in our past strategies and behaviours. We become objective. We look at our behavioural patterns as the mother looks at her baby. Strange, but familiar.

After the birth, life proceeds and learning continues. A mother learns about her new baby. She manages the routine, takes decisions and controls the boundaries of her relationship with her child. In the same way, a growing woman takes decisions, and controls her relationship boundaries. In both cases, separation and dis-identification are features of the process.

As the child grows, separation increases and greater autonomy is gained by the child – until, as a separate being, she gives birth to her own child. The cycle goes on.

Although, like all babies, the women in this study were born with their beauty and potential in tact, during their growing years, they were weighed down with other people's baggage until they couldn't see themselves any more. Although they all had the natural impetus to grow and expand their personalities, this was impeded by their childhood experiences and, just as a plant seeking light bends and twists, their personalities became distorted and hide the truth of who they were. However, 'a secret unrest gnaws at the roots of our being' and we cannot be held at bay forever. As it became increasingly impossible to ignore the gnawing, the women could no longer contain themselves and they literally burst out of their restrictive behaviours. Finally, they were born to themselves.

Revelation and becoming

Psychologists believe that the process of growing in maturity and wisdom is a revelatory process by which a woman drops the protective masks which have enabled her to face life. As we know, we use masks to protect ourselves and this is quite healthy – up to the point where the mask becomes our reality. Heather talked of 'the bit of me that never came out' as she discussed the roles she could put on and take off in the different compartments of her life. Although donning and removing masks sounds simple enough, it can be quite threatening to face the world without the mask you have relied upon in the past to protect yourself. When you remove a mask, your vulnerabilities are exposed and the way you engage in relationship with others is no longer clear. However, engaging with the possibility, and experiencing the fear of dropping your mask, enables you to discover the unknown elements of yourself. So clearly, it is worth working through your natural resistance and experimenting in relatively controlled environments at the beginning.

In the safety and freedom of a good therapeutic relationship, you may find that your resistance and your fears can be experienced and let go so that you are somewhat prepared for facing the world more authentically. And, the more you present yourself authentically to the world, the more you will reveal to yourself about yourself. And, the more you reveal about yourself to yourself, the more your decisions and choices will reflect who you are, what you need and what you want. At this point, you will no longer define yourself through others, nor will you take on the alien attitudes and behaviours of others. Instead, you'll become 'who you are'.

When we give ourselves over to another, we diminish ourselves. To add our brightness to someone else's light certainly magnifies them, but it reduces us. Of course, people love being round those who make them feel bigger, better and brighter, but it is energy draining for us and it denies our own richness and beauty. If we give our light to someone else, we end up denying something of ourselves and, if we deny aspects of ourselves for too long, a kind of pressure builds up that eventually leads to an explosion of expression. This can be really surprising for those who happen to be around when the eruption occurs as it is seen to be 'out of character'. In fact, it is entirely 'in character', but a hidden aspect of the character that has been suppressed for years and not been allowed out. So, women who deny their needs or qualities over a long period of time are really building up pressure that will need to be released at some point. If it doesn't happen before, it often happens in mid-life when some radical and unexpected behaviours are suddenly expressed that appear reckless and foolish. Women leave home, build exciting but dangerous relationships, embark on new careers and experience and express different things. It is both sad and wonderful that this should happen. Sad because there have been years when they have lived a reduced life, denying themselves and those close to them the full glory of who they are. Wonderful, because at last the full potential of who they are can be released and find expression.

After the early, and sometimes less than dignified eruption, women generally find a way to put their newfound fullness to use and learn to live with it graciously and authentically. But we are each doing it on our own and struggling to find the way as if the path had never been trodden before. So, instead of re-inventing the process each time, perhaps we can tap into the known dynamics and challenges that the process offers and learn to support and guide each other as we go through it. We could do this by forming a supportive and honouring network that others can access to get help as they negotiate the transitions and transformations that they will almost inevitably be invited to experience. By sharing our understanding of the process, by offering support and attentive listening, we can assist the release of women's creative potential beyond all that has so far been achieved.

Dropping our masks is not the full extent of becoming whole and it is not as easy as it sounds. This merely reveals aspects of ourselves which have not encountered the outside world before and, because of this, they can be over-sensitive and vulnerable. Recognising this, it is important to find surrogate masks that enable you to bring your vulnerabilities to the fore safely. One of the ways of doing this is to use other channels of transformation that are available to you such as the creative, kinaesthetic or spiritual channels. All these transformative channels release and direct energy around the mind and body as if it were a cool summer breeze refreshing stale air. Practically, this means going for a massage or complementary healing therapy, running, dancing, painting, singing and so on. These are powerful transforming activities that complement the inevitable intellectual activity that accompanies transformation.

Staying with the notion of energy, it is also crucial to release anger, perhaps more helpfully seen as blocked energy. This doesn't necessarily mean thrashing about and hitting things, although it may, it means unplugging the blockage and allowing the anger to escape fully without being replenished again. As emotions are the fuel for anger, it is no surprise that anger release uses the emotions in some way – but you can be inventive about how you do this.

Talking about anger without qualifying what it means, however, can be misleading because anger is not always a visible, passionate, high energy, expression. It can sit at the root of our personality and just pollute things quietly and generally. We may have a negative disposition, a strict set of rules that we don't like people breaking or a cynical, sarcastic or biting humour. We may put ourselves down a lot or resent other people's lives and successes. Or we may feel that the world is against us and something is conspiring to make us miserable. None of these forms of expression are blatantly rooted in anger in the sense that they are expressed physically in the heat of the moment. Instead, they are slow burring, smouldering undermining attitudes that reduce the quality and enjoyment of life. If this describes the way you face the world, try to go to the source of these feelings. Unpick them and ask yourself what core belief you hold that causes this set of responses. If you do this successfully, you'll probably find an injustice or a trespass that you haven't dealt with so you just keep feeding it with evidence that it's true and reinforcing it through an 'I told you so!' orchestration of your experiences and observations.

Of course, it is not always easy to identify the source of your anger but if you ask someone close to you, they may be able to link up your comments about the world and pinpoint the beliefs that you hold implicitly. This kind of feedback is always helpful, if not a little painful, because you will not be allowed to escape the fact that you are the one constantly feeding your own anger and keeping it alive. But by recognising this and revisiting the source of your anger you will find a way to let it go. Once exposed, it is very difficult to hold on to anger wantonly!

You will not have to rely solely on your own powers of analysis to move you through the transformative process. Unseen and formerly untapped internal resources will be brought to the fore quite naturally. These are the resources that are held in your subconscious mind but nevertheless find a way of rising to offer assistance when it is most needed. By listening to and tapping into your wisdom, therefore, you will be led safely through your process. You may access this wisdom through your spiritual practice or you may enter stillness and hear it through the thoughts that bubble up in your silence. However you do it, you'll be accessing your wisdom intuitively and transcending the rational thoughts that you hold in your mind. Sometimes, you will be led to do something that is apparently irrational and sits in opposition to what you believe to be wise or true, but go there and see where it takes you. It is not just rational clarity that you are seeking now, nor is it merely a means of survival, it is an expression of something much deeper.

You are on the way to a different way of being with yourself honestly and genuinely and, by taking and applying the wisdom that stems from your unconscious, you will arrive at a fullness of expression which will thrive in the open space that you have created for it.

Just now, you may be in at the beginning stages of your journey or you may be well down the track and expressing more of your authenticity and truth than ever before. This may be a transformative journey that you have expressly chosen or you may have been thrown at it unwillingly. Wherever you are and whatever you are doing, you will probably be able to look back already and see the steps that you have taken laid out behind you. If you do this for a moment, think about what triggered your first step; the waking stage. You may recognise that your trigger attempted to send you on your way many times before. It may have come in different forms and at different times to invite you to take the journey but perhaps it was too much, too soon. Somewhere inside, you would have known that it would be an arduous journey and you may have wanted to postpone it for a while, or deny that it was your path altogether! But the trigger or 'call to adventure' doesn't give up when you have more to offer. You have been called to reveal yourself fully. (In some ways, ignoring your wake-up call is not a waste of time. You may have rejected it outright but it will not have escaped the notice of your subconscious mind which will have been processing deeply ever since; a kind of latent preparation that will bring you to the point of choosing to go on the journey after all.)

What many women dread about the journey on an unconscious level, although they wouldn't necessarily be able to articulate this dread, is the next stage of the process which is marked by 'the fall'. This is the chaotic or fragmented stage of the journey. This is where there is a sense that everything is falling apart, control is lost and nothing makes sense any more.

If you take up the challenge of the journey, you are very likely to feel like a stranger in a strange land and you won't even be able to speak the language! After overcoming the feelings of foreboding and a strong resistance to setting off on the journey at all, the women described their first response to the challenges they met. Sometimes, they entered a deep sadness or depression; sometimes they described an almost physical sensation of things coming undone and control slipping from their grasp, but they also talked about experiencing a sense of loss. Their sense of loss occurred because they no longer had a known context. This brought up feelings of confusion and disorientation because their routines and responses were not relevant in the ambiguity of their new world. But it was not just the absence of a known context that created their sense of loss; it was much more personal than that. Their sense of loss was exacerbated by the fact that they had lost something of their former personality; the person they had known themselves to be; the person who had enacted their former routines and responses. They had literally lost their old self but they hadn't yet found their new self. They were in a kind of limbo where structure and substance had been swept away along with themselves. Often this stage is experienced as a bereavement and, although no-one has actually died, the sense will be that of a death; the death of the old self. The good news is that after death, comes a birth. It's just that you can't see it yet and you can't see the fact that the birth will necessarily and absolutely be a being that will be fulsome in her potential and personality.

Anyway, as you gird yourself with courage and continue on your way, you will move into a phase on the journey where you will need to find your voice and be heard. This is the signal that you are progressing along the path and literally giving voice to yourself; you are speaking yourself into being. In doing this, you give yourself anchor points which enable you to test out what you think in a tangible and practical way. You are laying down the foundations of a new structure that will create meaning for you in the next phase of your life and it will be uniquely characterised by you. Finding someone to talk to, whether it be a counsellor, therapist or friend, allows your voice to be heard and your truths to be surfaced. By having these witnessed, you learn to know yourself better. When you hear yourself articulate the thoughts that are held in the deepest recesses of your mind, you can look at them objectively, ask yourself if they are meaningful to you and decide whether or not you want to discard or keep them. You can also adjust, change or refine them so that they carry the precise expression of who you are at the present time.

Carl Rogers is an advocate of client-centred therapy, an approach which is predicated on the belief that the client holds within herself, answers to the questions and dilemmas that she is experiencing. At this stage on your journey it is you that holds the key, and the client-centred approach allows you to find it and turn it. By facilitating an examination of what's happening in your mind through making an empathic connection, listening attentively and being in non-judgement, a therapist can help you give birth to yourself and witness you build meaning. And, by getting your head around the situation and reflecting on your assumptions and beliefs, you will begin to gather momentum. In fact, at this stage, you are probably past one of the most challenging and potentially debilitating stages on your journey because if you don't find your voice and start making sense of your situation, you are in danger of living in ambiguity or chaos for a long time - perhaps for ever!

I well remember an article in the local paper about a widow who died in her late eighties leaving a home and possessions that were stuck 60 years in the past. She had lived a reclusive life and had no family to speak of. She had been happily married as a young woman, until 60 years ago, she and her husband had decided to go for a picnic one sunny Sunday afternoon in spring. She had packed a hamper and they had taken their car to the countryside where they enjoyed their picnic. After lunch they took a stroll in the woods and picked an armful of bluebells. She had placed the bluebells on the back seat of the car as they set off for home. Shortly, they arrived home and put the car in the garage but before they had had a chance to unpack its contents, her husband had a massive heart attack and died. She was so devastated that she shut the garage door and never went in it again. She also shut the front door behind her, shut the world out of her life and lived in her grief until she herself died 60 years later. When the house was opened, it was exactly as it had been all those years earlier, the utilities, the décor, the furniture and the kitchen equipment. And the car, now a vintage, was still in the garage with the dried up bluebells on the back seat. This woman had lived in her grief for the whole of her life. She had never found new meaning. She had never found her voice and she had never been witnessed. Her life turned to stone. She merely existed until she finally died all those years later. This is one of the most poignant stories of 'stuckness' that I have heard and it chills me to think of the sadness that that woman must have endured for so long.

Meaning-making is primarily, but not exclusively, driven by the mind and involves deep levels of thinking and contemplation. By using critical reflection and voice, it is possible to review and re-work the values and assumptions you have carried through your life until this point. During this time, you have an opportunity to jettison the belief structures that were given to you by your parents, teachers or other significant people in your formative years. Again, assuming that all of us are wounded in our childhoods, we are bound to have to rethink this wounding and find a different way of seeing it and a different way of responding to it. It has conditioned our lives and has brought us to a place of transformation and it is time to let it go and find out what we really think and what we really want from our lives.

Too much intellectualisation can be counterproductive. For many in the study, intellectualisation was a coping strategy that was adopted as a protective mechanism. It prevented the need to face the trauma but it also perpetuated the behaviours that were created in response to the trauma in the first place. Being stuck in the head can eclipse the many other channels of transformation and become a displacement activity that stops the 'real work' from taking place. In cases of over-intellectualisation, the mind tries to make sense of that which is senseless. It goes round and round as it tries to rationalise the irrational behaviours of people from our pasts and the feelings that emerged in response to these. But there is no logic to feeling and the mind can never work it out. As rational beings, a contradiction in terms if ever there was one, we often try to make our heads rule our hearts - but we equally often fail.

Although I have stressed the importance of critical reflection to help us create meaning, I must say again that this activity is most powerful when it is balanced by our feelings and emotions. Thoughts and feelings need to be accessed simultaneously if the full extent of the process is to be experienced. Indeed, using both the head and the heart is vital if life itself is to be experienced in full.

Once you have laid down the head and heart foundations for yourself in your new world, you will need to train those in relationship to you to respond to you differently. If you can do this, you will be able to establish and reinforce yourself in your new guise. This means setting boundaries and demonstrating commitment to the person you are becoming; more autonomous and more distinctive in your being. Inevitably, this will lead to some relationships falling out of your network whilst others will arrive. As you change your own terms of engagement, people will choose whether or not they wish to accept them; even intimate relationships. Sadly, sometimes we lose closeness with family members and partners who have come to rely upon our dysfunctional consistency and who are judging what we are doing against the level of disturbance to their lives. And, if they aren't prepared to, or able to, go with us into our process, the reward for being with us will diminish and they will seek others to feed their needs. They probably won't go without a fight though. You are likely to be tested with 'are you sure you're prepared to pay the price of losing me?!' type challenges and you will need to be resolute in your determination to bring yourself into full being. It may sound harsh but to compromise yourself at this stage is saying that others are worth more than you are; that their needs are greater than yours and that you need to hold yourself back in order to serve them. (Of course, if you have young children, you may not feel that you have the same degree of choice that others with no children or a grown family may have. But you will still have choices and you can still orchestrate your world differently and in accord with your own evolution.)

During this stage of the process, most of the women found that quite a few of their close relationships changed. Some of them left their partners to live alone, others found new partners. Some experimented with their sexual orientation whilst others sought many and varied hetero-sexual experiences. Some entered unknown territory explicitly and travelled freely whilst others created a safe space for themselves. This stage is all about controlling your environment and choosing how you want to occupy it. It relies upon you knowing instinctively what you need and using your intuition to guide you through. You are now beginning to tap into your unique female resources and use your talents to shape your life. It is a powerful place to be.

Finding a suitable place to put your thoughts and experiences, and re-jigging your values and beliefs, is really an ongoing process that pervades all other stages. And, as you accumulate more and more knowledge, the web of meaning that you create will expand to accommodate it. In fact, it will eventually get so large that it will be able to hold the tension between opposites. You can be both emotional and rational, for instance, without denying the truth of either. You can be both loving and critical, both happy and sad, the 'life and soul' and the 'wallflower'. When your meaning mesh becomes this large, your perspective on life is much more accepting. And, because your perspective is so great, the 'rules' no longer hold true; there are no absolutes.

No change can take place without you absorbing and integrating your wider observations and allowing yourself to accept and flow with them. When you do this, you are increasing your boundaries of tolerance and freeing yourself from self-imposed restrictions and limitations. Indeed, you will find that you are coping more easily with the complexity of life and allowing it to flow past you without getting caught up in its current. It is now that you can become non-attached and secure in your own being. It is now that you get a sense of renewal and a stronger sense of Self. And it will be generative; the more you feel it, the more you'll get of it.

Whenever you move from one life stage to another, you build new meaning to accommodate the change. It is a natural process that we see at work, perhaps most visibly, as infants move into adolescence and challenge the dependency/control boundary. Or as adolescents move into adulthood and challenge the control/responsibility boundary. These transitions always involve moving form an emphasis on one quality to embracing another. Moving from a dependent infant to taking control as a teenager for instance. Or migrating from a controlling adolescent to taking responsibility as an adult. Just as a runner in a relay race deliberately and decisively hands the baton over to the next runner, life transitions deliberately and decisively hand over increasing levels of self-responsibility and self-definition. It is an emergent process that results in freer more accepting behaviours that do not attach to those things over which we have no control or influence. We become increasingly fluid in our personalities and increasingly able to manage complexity and contradiction. As we age and as our life experiences grow, we are deliberately and decisively propelled towards an expansion of consciousness, and, if we are doing it according to the plan, we grow in wisdom.

It is clear that integrating is not a final resting place however; it is both a foundation for the next phase of growth and a part of it. Transcendence is what happens when you are able to look back, appraise the journey and talk about it without an emotional attachment to it. This is not the same as being unemotional, instead it is the ability to understand and act on the fact that the emotions are no longer current. To re-feel them is to go back into the pain and re-experience it. There is no need for that. Transcending is when you cast a dispassionate eye over a landscape that you have travelled but left behind. It gives you perspective and freedom to turn and continue the next leg of your journey. It is during this final stage that authenticity is found, no masks, no hiding; you are liberated to be yourself.

As always, there is good news and bad news as you finish your journey. You have triumphed, emerged wiser, freer, happier – only to start again. Three is no end to the journey of life. It just keeps on going, inviting you to higher and higher levels of wisdom and greater expressions of who you are. But there are high spots and this is certainly one. Rest here for as long as you reasonably can and take pride and joy in your achievements. You have revealed more of your potential and beauty than ever before.

The Challenge for Women today

I have spoken to many women now, who are meeting the challenges of their growth into fully functioning, conscious and choosing people; who are seeking to express their full potential expansively and joyously and who are seeking to access their womanhood. Mostly, these women have trodden a path that was conditioned for them, either by their family or by society. They have been 'good girls' and have played by the rules that enabled them to survive in one kind of world or another – either professionally or personally. Not only this, but they have been encouraged to straddle the chasm between the two without losing their female qualities, and made to feel as if they have failed if they haven't succeeded in doing so with all the ease and sexual prowess of Superwoman!

Women today are on the cusp of defining a new place for themselves; they sit on the fulcrum of change and there are few role models to assist them in their quest for full expression. Visions of health and beauty are dangled before us in magazines and women at the top of their professional trees are written about admiringly. Mothering is an expected and prized quality in a woman along with a flair for housewifery, cookery and sex. Romance and marriage still hold a fascination for many and celebrity examples, although both inspiring and appalling at times, are compelling reflections for us to measure ourselves against. But these are winner takes all examples of success and few manage to combine all the elements of a full life with ease and grace. Yet that's the challenge that many of us are unwittingly taking on.

I have heard women talk of the confusion they feel in the milieu that is modern culture and modern relationship. To what extent can they extend their boundaries into territory that has not been their preserve in the past? Too much and there is push back from the men. Too little and there is criticism that they are not contributing their talent. To what extent can they occupy traditional female territory? Too much and their importance tends to be overlooked. Too little and they are considered to be deficit. And, whilst these see-saw dynamics plot out a contorted path, women are looking for their authenticity; not that bestowed upon them by their parents or significant others, but the truth of who they are; their inner core. This must be likened to a cake walk, where a step onto what appears to be firm ground turns out to be thin air, and where a step into what appears to be thin air sees the ground rushing up to slap you in the face.

I'm not trying to make a case for the impossibility of women expressing their various and extensive talents, but trying to acknowledge how hard it is and how much courage is needed to stand up in truth and say 'this is who I am'. We are in uncharted territory. We are still emerging from the drag effect of the war years where choice of product, circumstance or role was considered to be a luxury and for which extreme amounts of gratitude had to be expressed. And, for most of us, it is a world of plenty; a world where we have the power and technology to create our own reality and our own fortunes. We are also encouraged to take risks and find the edge of our potential yet we are held in hostile accountability for being different. How then, do we bounce meaningfully between all these opposing worlds whilst holding on to our integrity, dignity and truth? How do we step beyond the pull of the archetype that has defined the role of lover, mother and wife for generations without incurring disappointment or wrath? These are the issues, along with career and financial management, along with childcare, along with relationship, along with ongoing education and technological advancement that we are trying to grapple with. How can we fathom our female truth in all of this? No wonder there's confusion!

I had a call from a good friend recently. She is in her fifties, a retired teacher, divorced from her alcoholic husband, and a mother of two children who have both grown up and left home. She trained to be a healer but her practice is sketchy and periodic and unlikely to deliver the professional focus that would create meaning for her in her mature years. She has no intimate relationship. Eventually, she sold her home and took to the air. She has travelled extensively. Mongolia, Egypt, India,

Australia, North and South America as well as every corner of Europe. She has sought spiritual inspiration through teachers, healers and gurus in these various places and has put a great deal of energy into answering the one question that she feels ill equipped to answer, 'Who am I?'. You'd think that this protracted journey would bring her some realisations; an understanding and affection for the person that she carries within her, but all that her outward searching has achieved is to reinforce the void she feels inside and leave her breathless and bewildered. "Dena", she said when I picked up the phone, "I just don't know who I am any more." No longer the wife. No longer the mother. No longer the teacher. No longer the healer. Every 'no longer' cutting still more ground from beneath her feet until she was left standing on a mole-hill, precariously, wondering where the foundations were and what she could use as a touchstone.

Perhaps she had taken an outer journey; a valuable journey that revolved her slowly until she was facing herself and ready to ask the question 'Who am I?' Perhaps now it is time to venture inward; to dig deep, reflect on her exotic experiences and draw a golden thread through her responses and reactions to the situations she found herself in. Perhaps it is reflection and integration that is needed now and not another extra-ordinary adventure. I do not wish to be trite when I suggest this, just to recognise that there are different ways and different modes of journeying and, if we choose the 'wrong' mode, we are in danger of staying in the same place with the same questions unanswered whilst we distract ourselves with activity.

Another friend of mine, who is newly out of a marriage which was also a business partnership, is trying to forge her own path and find her place and direction as an independent woman. She has all round capability, strength and determination and doesn't know which of her talents to focus on or how to channel it productively. "What ever I do now says something about me and I want it to be true! I want to be seen as myself, not as a sad, single person struggling to get by until the next relationship poles up. So what is it I want to do? I just don't know which way to turn." For her and so many of us, we are seeking to combine our male and female aspects and mix a delightful cocktail that carries the distinctive flavour of all worlds. Female intuition, sensuality and wisdom coupled with male capability, focus and success. It is new, this thing that we seek. There are few that have managed it even to their fleeting satisfaction.

And all this is without even touching on the female form and how we feel about our bodies. I don't know one woman, nor have I met one in my work or research who accepts, let alone loves, her body. We barrel towards the change points in our lives with distaste for what we have and despair about ever getting what we think we don't have. Too fat. Too thin. To tall. Too short. Inelegant. Out of balance. Ugly. As well, we measure ourselves against screen sirens that have sexuality, sensuality, mystery, intrigue and power. Of course, there have been high profile stabs at trying to get us to accept our bodies through famous but 'spherically challenged' images of contentment and happiness, but actually, they fall on deaf ears. We still strive for physical and sexual perfection and judge ourselves harshly when we do not measure up. Am I exaggerating to make my point? I hope so, but I don't think so. We may be happy with some of our attributes; intellectual, physical, emotional, spiritual and sexual, but there always seems to be space to beat ourselves up about something. And, when and if we succeed in dealing with that, something else emerges to suck away our energy and confidence. But beauty really does lie in the eyes of the beholder, and we must behold ourselves, within and without, to experience our beauty. This is the route to self-acceptance. By knowing who we are, by knowing our beauty, we can become bold advocates for ourselves and find joy in our unique expression. There is nothing more glorious than a woman in her truth.

Yet, the hardest thing in the world is to know oneself. Zen Buddhist monks reflect on Koans for a lifetime; these are the imponderable eternal questions such as 'What is the sound of one hand clapping?' and more currently, 'Who am I?' which must be the oldest question known to humankind. Deep thinkers and spiritual practitioners adopt yogic reflective practice to drop into the deepest part of themselves and Enlightenment Intensives create a hothouse environment where personal enlightenment is possible. Brandon Bays, in her book *The Journey*, offers a framework for answering this question, which relies, like the Enlightenment Intensive, on two people working together and continuously focusing on the question 'Who am I?' I am not outlining these practices to daunt you, but to suggest that what you are doing, what you *have* to do, is difficult. Perhaps, in some way, this will encourage you to stay with the ambiguity and allow it to take you to your truth. It is only by letting go of who you thought you were that you will find out who you really are. As we are so often told, you can't make an omelette without cracking the eggs. It is the egg-cracking that is so hard, but it releases such rich food. For you, the 'egg shell' may be the values and beliefs that you were given as a child, the 'rules' that held you securely and fashioned your life, the meaning mesh that helped you make sense of your observations and experiences. All this needs to be released, re-thought and reconstructed – again and again – and in doing this, you will find the essence of yourself.

Our challenge, as women then, is to wade through the distractions of the world, the theme park exhilaration and the sound-bite wisdom and find our core essences; the people we *really* are deep inside. It is only then that we can add our weight to the collective shoulder that is pushing to change the order of things and enhance everyone's life experience. Our creativity, inspiration, intuition, sensitivity, beauty – all this and more is waiting to be released as we journey into the heart of ourselves and reveal the energy and potential that lies within.

But in today's social environment, overshadowed by the archetypes of which I have spoken, we often commit to relationships, bright and earnest in the expectation that they will deliver us into our happy ever after fantasy. But in reality, these youthful dreams cannot contain us through all the adult phases of our life and on to Cronedom. It is so hard to loosen or shed the responsibilities of our relationships for the sake of our own interests. It is perceived to be selfish, destructive and unkind. How do women pull their feet from this mud-sucking expectation that they will be companions and nurturers for ever? How do they bring their partners with them or sever their relationships so that they are free to travel? So many women speak of this dilemma. Love has not gone. Concern and tenderness has not gone. But relationship and compatibility has gone. To wrench oneself away from the traditional roles and to reinterpret these imaginatively requires such courage and strength. There is another life to be had.

The former pattern of life stages has changed along with the increase in longevity that our society has gifted to us. Mid-life is the new thirties; a time for exploration and experimentation. It is a time to leave your imprint on the world. It is not a time for retirement – spiritually speaking at least – but a time to find and express yourself. In the course of my work, I have met women who sit on the knife-edge of committed relationship for years, sometimes twenty or more years, fearing the conse-quences of their own potential and the inevitability of a disruption in their domestic situation. This is a *real* dilemma. It clutches at the parts of us that 'know' we have more to experience and, at the same time, it pulls on our heart strings, especially if we see our loved ones in terms of their dependency upon us. There is no pat answer to this. It is for each of us to work out in our own way. But it does highlight the battle that we face between 'truth' and 'service'.

By way of inspiration, let me share with you my own mother's victory of self-expression. As a young woman in a country fresh from war, she married an army officer. He offered all the virtues of safety and security to a young woman whose formative years had been battle scarred. Not only was a war raging but also she was sent away to school for her own safety and enjoyed only a sad facsimile of family life. As a young woman in the early 1950s, marriage was an optimistic avenue and she took it. However, she was a creative eccentric. He a structured intellectual. It was not an unhappy union, but there was no room for creative eccentricity in the context of the English army. After three children, two grand children and thirty years of artistic and spiritual frustration, she fled. It was a brave act. Now, if I could hold a drop of my mother's essence up for you to see, you would be dazzled by a radiant example of fulfilment and joy. Always busy. Always curious. Always loving and interesting, she has found herself. And, along with buckets of inspiration and energy, she has helped others find themselves too. It is never too late. If you go to Glastonbury, you'll find her there, shining. In some way, and in honour of those who do, we absolutely must let the seepage that disquiets our soul turn into a torrent of self-expression.

So, on the fulcrum of your own truth, as you balance all the conundrums of the modern world, cast your eyes around and see where and how you wish to participate. Watch for the signals that cue your entry. Fan the flames of change, make it your agenda. There is not 'right' and 'wrong' any more. There is just your truth.

Finally

At the outset of my research study, I had aspirations of identifying a process and of creating a route map that would assist women as they explored their inner landscape. I thought, if they had some sort of guide, it would help them travel and meet their challenges knowingly and effectively. I also hoped that its impact would be felt in the counselling arena where knowledge about the transformative process of healing would inform the way a counsellor or therapist accompanied a client. However, I later came to appreciate that, although it is possible to build such a map, it is not possible to short-circuit the route and protect people from the necessity of their own experiences. It can, however, act as a valuable set of reference points for travellers and counsellors and provide them with the wherewithal to take stock when the going gets tough.

The qualities that you need to take with you are awareness, intention and attention, each one being over-lighted by vision and courage. Awareness, intention and attention are focusing qualities that enable you to clarify your goals and marshal the various creative energies that need to be harnessed to get you there. Without these qualities, all your energies will be dissipated and lost in vague attempts to effect some form of movement. Just as a team of horses has to pull in the same direction to make progress, so does your energy and determination. You must know your destination and take responsibility for providing the forward propulsion to get yourself there. The way in which you experience this journey, however, will differ from the experience of another. They will meet the same challenges differently as well as meet different challenges. For this reason, we can refer to those that have travelled the path and we can draw from their experiences but we cannot have them travel for us. A comparison can be drawn with childbirth or falling in love. Although much is written about these processes, there is no way of circumventing the experience and reaching an early and painless conclusion based upon informed advice from others. The process must be experienced first hand in order for us to arrive at a point where we can identify and concur with others' interpretation of the process. Although the old adage, 'forewarned is forearmed' may not apply in this case, some comfort may be gained by knowing that the process is transitory, has its own wisdom and will take you where you need to go.

As I near the end of this book, I find I am reflecting more deeply on the research, analysis and writing processes and how they have each affected me. Perhaps unsurprisingly, I feel that I have experienced a transformative process as a result of taking this project from conception to closure. At the outset, I was objective in my approach and believed that I would proceed along the well-trodden academic route, arriving at the other end with a neatly packaged theory that would inform both my, and others' understanding. I did not anticipate the personal depths that I would plumb nor did I anticipate the process changing me in any way. But how could I have come out unscathed having sat with the women as they related their experiences and having listened to the recordings with an empathetic ear'? These activities, along with the transcription and analysis of their words, have brought me close to an amazing group of women. Through their stories, I have found a connection that I hadn't anticipated and a resonance that dug deep. At the same time, I had to distance myself from them so that I could hear their words and understand their meaning without the warm cloak of friendship blurring my thinking. Now, as time removes me from our encounter, I can only offer them my admiration, respect and gratitude for allowing me to take some steps alongside them for a while.

Looking back, I had great reluctance to be critical of other theorists' work and differentiate myself from them. In my respect for intellectuals and academics (not believing for an instant that I was one), I was consumed by the inevitable correctness of their work and the relative futility of my own – a stance that is bewilderingly antithetical to undertaking original research. I was constantly seeking validation through others' work and dismantling my own convictions as I shielded my eyes, ears and senses against my findings. I was attempting to do something distinctive, yet instead of highlighting the *difference* between my thinking and theirs, I sought *similarity*. In truth, when I thought about it deeply, I found that I was fearful of difference because it would force me to stand alone and be disconnected from those I respected; a troublesome place for me to stand. It was with great effort that I pulled myself from this mire to engage with the uniqueness of my work. As if this wasn't transformative enough, I realised too that I was struggling to mould a theory using others' thinking structures, techniques and styles and that *I* was not being reflected in my words. Indeed, I was hidden somewhere beneath the surface which I hoped would appear polished, elegant, thoughtful and 'correct'. Although my ambitions for the finished product remained unaltered, I had to return to the text time and again and reintroduce myself to the words so that I could weave my own thread through the writing. This was not a piece of work that I could hide behind; nor could I be invisible in presenting it. And so I reclaimed my authority and opened to my intuition and wisdom, allowing them to flood into the work in order to bring illumination to a messy, conflicting and contradictory process that is undergone by many to varying degrees of success.

Having come to the end of this book, you will now know who I am. I have revealed myself in my thinking, my analysing and my writing. I stand by my findings but I make no claims of correctness. My interpretation of the process is not *the* truth, it is merely my view and I hope, deeply, that it will stimulate debate, bring insights and assist those passing over the transformative terrain. This has certainly been a transformative experience for me and I feel that I have arrived at a new place of self-knowledge – but not the ultimate place. It has been unexpectedly difficult to write these words and the trials have been many but I rest in gratitude that these transformative processes are part of the human experience and trust that they will continue to play out in life to bring advancement and richness to the world.

These finals words were written on the day Pope John Paul II died, 2nd April 2005. I turn to him for my final quotation:

'Suffering is the crucible where one's humanity emerges in its greatness; in the ability to overcome suffering with hope and joy, and serenity.'

(Monsignor Lorenzo Albacete speaking on behalf of his friend, Pope John Paul II)

Postscript

After I had been awarded my PhD I travelled to Ireland to see Mata Amritanandamayi, often referred to as Amma or Ammachi, meaning 'Mother'. (See www.ammachi.org) Amma is believed to be a manifestation of the Divine Mother. Amma came from humble beginnings in a small village in Kerala, Southern India, and travels the world and receives many people for Darshan (a meeting with a holy person). She gives Darshan through an embrace during which she conveys compassion and unconditional love. Many feel healed as a result of her embrace, some gain personal insights, others rest in her expression of love and are deeply moved by the experience. In the past 30 years, she has embraced over 21 million people throughout the world, has paid for and presided over many humanitarian projects, provided food and shelter for many thousands of people without personal resources of their own and educated many more thousands of young people in modern technology, medicine and management. When I arrived at the venue in Ireland, footage of Amma was being shown on a screen that acted as a back-drop to the Darshan activity. In the excerpt I was watching, Dr Jane Goodall had presented Amma with the 2002 Gandhi-King Award for Non-violence at the Global Peace Initiative of Women Religious and Spiritual Leaders. Her acceptance speech had a profound impact on me and seemed to emphasise the importance of disseminating any findings that would help women find their authenticity and power; their 'being'.

I reproduce some of her speech here:

'Women in countries where materialism is predominant should awaken to spirituality [knowing oneself and realising the infinite power within]... It has been widely believed that women and the cultures in which they live will awaken through education and material development. But time has taught us that this concept is too limited. Only when women imbibe the eternal wisdom of the spiritual, along with modern education, will the power within them awaken -

and they will rise to action... No external power can possibly obstruct woman or her innate qualities... such as love, empathy and patience. It is she ... who has to awaken herself. A woman's mind is the only real barrier that prevents this from happening.

Women should let go of their fear and distrust, they are simply illusions. The limitations women think they have are not real. Women need to muster the strength to overcome those imagined limitations. They already possess this power; it is right here and once that power has been evoked, no one will be able to stop the forward march of women in every area of life.

A wrong beginning set on a faulty foundation is one of the reasons why women lose out so much in life. It isn't only that women should share equal status with men in society; the problem is that women are given a bad start in life due to wrong understanding and lack of proper awareness. So women are trying to reach the end without the benefit of having the beginning.

Women are the power and the very foundation of our existence in the world. When women lose touch with their real selves, the harmony of the world ceases to exist and destruction sets in. It is therefore crucial that women everywhere make every effort to rediscover their fundamental nature, for only then, can we save this world.'

Mata Amritanandamayi, 2002

On the occasions that I have been embraced by Amma, I have experienced complete love and joy. As I lie in her arms, and as her heart opens to me, and mine to her, I am immersed in a feeling of relief and gratitude. It may have something to do with acceptance of each other as sisters in spirit or with being in the flow of undiluted love. Whatever it is, it is refreshing, re-energising and expanding. Amma is a remarkable role model; endlessly working for the spiritual evolution and transformation of humanity, but with a particular emphasis on the female qualities of that she calls 'universal motherhood'. She is a great advocate of women, and, incidentally, she is also an advocate of the emergence of the qualities of universal motherhood in men. There can be no more credible woman alive who can challenge people everywhere to become all that they can be.

Footnotes

[1] Firman, John. and Gila, Ann. (1997) *The Primal Wound: a transpersonal view of trauma, addiction and growth.* State University of New York Press (1997: pp 1-2)

[2] Myss, Caroline. (1997) *Anatomy of the Spirit: the seven stages of power and healing.* Bantam Books

[3] Kushner, Harold. (1981) *When Bad Things Happen to Good People.* Schocken Books: New York

[4] Krystal, Phyllis. (1993) *Cutting the Ties That Bind: growing up and moving on.* Red Wheel/Weiser.

[5] Virtue, Doreen PhD. (1997) *The Lightworker's Way: awakening your spiritual power to know and heal.* Hay House Inc: (1997: pp 220-221)

[6] Tolle, Eckhart (2004) *The Power of Now: a guide to spiritual enlightenment.* New World Library

[7] Campbell, Joseph (1993) *The Hero with a Thousand Faces.* Fontana Press: London (1993: pp 40)

[8] Dante Alighieri (1998) *The Divine Comedy.* Oxford World's Classics paperback

p29
p 26-p27 meaning mesh rather than meaning perspective
Be aware of thoughts
last para 1st
p 64, 65
p 81. p 84 excellent

p114 still lines) p115 paragraph 3, p116 esp face
p117 Bottom page p118 and 122, beginning 123
p134 appetive, honour yourself
p168 Dante 2wi/rc
p170 - in head etc
p171 - Ego
p 181, 182
Excellent authentically page 183 190
BOOKS
p 191, bitterness etc, resentment of others lives etc./
p193

p197,
198
199 wisdom
age
p 204, 205

O books

O is a symbol of the world, of oneness and unity. In different cultures it also means the "eye", symbolizing knowledge and insight, and in Old English it means "place of love or home". O books explores the many paths of understanding which different traditions have developed down the ages, particularly those today that express respect for the planet and all of life.

For more information on the full list of over 300 titles please visit our website
www.O-books.net